Among Myrtle Trees

written by
Christopher Paul Rees

Among the Myrtle Trees

Copyright © Christopher Paul Rees 2011

First Published December 2011
Published by Design Marque

Printed in Great Britain by
www.designmarque.co.uk

ACKNOWLEDGMENTS

I thank the members of Bethesda Baptist Chapel for their patience all these years and for giving me the privilege to serve them with the good news of Jesus Christ.

I especially mention Peter Preece who has encouraged me in writing this book and others who are unnamed in all their labours over the manuscript, but whose names and deeds are recorded in another book that will soon be opened and read before all.

Cover artwork Jean Murgatroyd and photographs by Alan Powditch.

During the night I had a vision – and there before me was a man riding a red horse! He was standing among the myrtle trees in the valley. Behind him were red, brown and white horses.
I asked, "what are these, my Lord?"
The angel who was talking with me answered, "I will show you what they are."
Then the man standing among the myrtle trees explained. "They are the ones the LORD has sent to go throughout the earth."

Zechariah 1 : 8 - 10

Printed in Wales by www.DesignMarque.co.uk

CONTENTS

High Street, Narberth

Introduction

Fiction reigns on the bookshelves. The literary world is awash with novels whose subjects are myth and legend, writings that take us into the unseen and make believe world. We live in a day when fiction is written as history and history as fiction. The book that fails to capture the reader's imagination is the one that simply records history as *history*. The worst one can do is to write the dullest of books (no matter how brief) by writing history as a catalogue of facts, dates, events and people without soul or imagination and without the stimulation of those ideas that turned our forefathers' world upside down. To miss something of the spirit that drove and influenced our ancestors to forsake all and follow Christ would be a great mistake.

History is always hard to pin down and so often can be seen as playing with dead men's bones, as Voltaire concluded. The problem in the relationship between fact and fable is even more acute when one writes of what may have happened in a place like Narberth. The history of the place and people is interwoven with legend. Land of the Mabinogion, the place where Druids ruled, a centre of Celtic tales, an ancient place where the supernatural and the natural are purported to have overlapped. The mythical tales of the Mabinogion speak of Arberth as the centre for Pwyll, Prince of Dyfed. Earliest history shows the influence of a pre–pagan people, descendants of Javan and of Japheth. The history of Narberth can be traced as far back as the Bronze and Iron Ages, with the actors in the drama being the Romans, Britons, Saxons, Normans and Flemings, and a story of might and magic, of racial ravages and social struggle. Living in Narberth, one soon learns that in such a community as this, legend and fable are believed by most and, as often is the case, fact is stranger than fiction.

I have painted the history of the Church in Narberth with a broad brush. However, this book deals with real people, with facts and events that can be traced to the foundation of the story and are from what can be, and has been, authenticated. The Christian faith is an historical faith. It is not a religion of fiction. It is a faith that proclaims that God is at work in this world, both in creation and salvation. History is seen as *His story*. The facts surrounding the life of Jesus Christ, as an historical person, can be verified beyond anyone else of that period. The spread of the Good News and the growth of the Church are recorded in Scripture and it is from this taproot that the Church took root in Narberth centuries ago.

Neglecting the past as we go into the future is a great mistake. To forget the Christian heritage that has been the bedrock of a healthy and prosperous community is something we can ill afford. As we celebrate the faithfulness of God in establishing and preserving the Baptist cause at Bethesda Chapel for two hundred years, the main focus of this narrative is given over to Bethesda's history. However, it has been impossible to write without reference to the other sections of the Christian Church that have played their part over the years in being a powerful witness to the Gospel, not only in this area but throughout the world. Hopefully, the theme of this book will be of interest not only to those of a particular denomination but to all Christians who love the cause of Christ - and even to those who may not have a faith but want to know the factors that have shaped the history of the community they live in.

This account illuminates not only the subject but also the landscape, people and events surrounding the story of Christianity in Narberth. It tells of the faith, courage and hope that our forefathers knew in the past and whose history would inspire us for the future.

As works of imagination, the historian's work and the novelist's do not differ.
Where they do differ is that the historian's is meant to be true.
R G Collingwood - The Idea of History

From the Woods They Came

The first glimpse of the Saviour came from the surrounding woods. Out of the woods they came, legions and armies into the valley. They had been coming to this spot for centuries. Some to hunt or conquer and others to retreat and hide away - but they came in the end to worship God. [1]

It was the Roman soldiers who first came, bringing with them a glimpse of His Person to these parts. They came, they saw, and they conquered. But, before they came to conquer the inhabitants of this principality, many of these soldiers had been conquered by the claims of the lonely and solitary Galilean Man, Jesus of Nazareth. It was soldiers from the Roman ranks that first enlisted to be soldiers for Christ's Army and Kingdom. From the commanders and the foot soldiers, to the elite palace guard,[2] to the champion fighters and heroes, many had pledged allegiance to Christ and given testimony to his Lordship in martyrdom. [3]

It was during the reign of Augustus Caesar that the Christ was born and under the Empire's power the sentence of crucifixion was pronounced and performed with the inscription *Jesus of Nazareth, King of the Jews.* The Apostolic Creed embeds the story of Christ in history, *Crucified under Pontius Pilate.* It was the Roman soldiers who beat Him and spat on Him. It was those from their ranks who hammered the nails into Him. It was the same hardened soldiers who gambled for His garments beneath the cross who, when they had seen the way the Christ died, proclaimed *truly this is the Son of God.* It was the same soldiers who had guarded the grave in vain. No power on earth could stop its stone being moved away because of the power of holiness that was at work in the tomb. The legions of Roman soldiers, even if they did not carry the news in their hearts, carried it on their lips as they now stood on the banks of the River Cleddau.

Julius Caesar landed on the shores of Britain in 55BC, but it was not for Julius to conquer the hearts of men and women. Long after Caesar had died, Tertullian could say, approximately 100 years after the New Testament Church, that Christianity had established itself in the remotest fringes of the Empire and had made it subject to the true Christ.

Origen, a contemporary of Tertullian, from the ancient city of Alexandria, could hammer home the joyous fact of the triumph of the Church in the land of Britannia. [4]

Local legend refers to the Emperor Magnus Maximus, who set up camp at the foot of Frennifawr as he came with his soldiers to those woods to hunt. It was on the bank of the River Cleddau at Cefen-Llwydarth that the last bear in Wales was killed. The Roman invaders had landed first on the shores of Kent in 43AD but it was not until 74AD that they came to the Welsh borders to make their conquest. The main western Roman fort was in the capital of the Demetae tribe at Carmarthen, some 30 miles east. [5]

The Romans never came to conquer the pagan religion of the Celtic people. It was never the policy of the Roman Empire to make a conquered people worship strange and unknown gods - and the last thing the superstitious Romans wanted to do was to anger the local deity whose land they now occupied. We cannot be sure as to what form Christianity took during those early years of the Roman occupation but it is clear that slowly but surely where those soldiers went it did grow. It was from the ranks of those soldiers that Aaron and Julius were martyred for their faith in the 3rd century. [6] However, this was only a glimpse of Christianity and for a short time. At the end of the 4th century, in 383AD, the legions left these lands, which then created a vacuum and an uncertain future.

Other invaders soon followed, the Saxons first from the east and Vikings a century later from the west. [7] These were troublesome times for the inhabitants of the land, with uncertainty and fear of barbaric foes to whom nothing was sacred. They did not, however, make it to this location, valley and forest. That was left for another army to conquer and settle. From the south, Brittany, and again from eastern Ireland they came but unlike the legions of Roman plunderers and raiders with their swords, spears, axes and clubs, there came an army of Saints with the weapons of preaching and prayer. They came to conquer the gods of pagan religion. With these Saints came a more powerful glimpse of the Saviour to these parts.

One by one, a host of Saints from Gaul settled in the forests of these mountains. Looking down on the sacred spot of Rhydwilym, you will find within three quarters of a mile and rising to over 300 feet above the valley at the top of Ffynonsamson, a well dedicated to Saint Samson of Brittany. From this point the little church of Llangolman can be seen, which was built as a result of the visit of St Colman to this part of the county. This was the *The Age of the Saints* and a time of great advancement when the message of Jesus Christ was taken to all parts of Wales.

Celtic Christianity in Wales was a movement that had strong links with the other Celtic nations. It was vibrant, monastic, evangelistic, educated, orthodox and independent of the Roman Church. It had its own leadership, with the greatest leader being the Patron Saint of Wales, David. His life has become legendary and there is one famous story of the ground rising under his feet as he addressed a church assembly at Llanddewi Brefi.What is significant about this story is that St David was warning against the teaching of Pelagianism, taught by another Welsh monk by the name of Morgan, teaching that mankind was able to obey the law of God without Grace or God's help. He denied the teaching of original sin: that mankind is born sinful because of Adam's fall and that man could live without sin. It was denounced as heresy. By contrast, St David stood for the Good News that speaks of the Grace of God towards mankind in its fallen condition. St David may be the Patron Saint of Wales but most of his work and influence was carried out with an itinerant ministry within a triangular circuit, from St David's to Llanddewi Brefi and Whitland. We can perhaps speculate that St David with his desire to share the Good News may have come to Narberth!

When Augustine, the first Archbishop of Canterbury, met the Celtic Bishops at Whitby in 603 he did not come to herald Christianity to these parts. Instead, he discovered a Church that had survived and developed since Roman times. The Celtic Church in Wales remained independent of the Roman Church in varying degrees for the next 400 years, clinging to its own practices long after other Celtic nations had yielded. A thousand years after Christ the Bible was known hereabouts, illustrating the Grace of God in providing a Saviour who had died on the cross for sinners. Saints had come to this valley, made their home in the woods and caves, and from here they went forth with the knowledge of His presence, the Risen Lord with God's saving news.

Be thou my vision, O Lord of my heart:
Nought be all else to me save that thou art;
Thou my Best thought, by day or by night,
Waking or sleeping, thy presence my light.

Irish Celtic Hymn of 8th Century

Deforestation

Bringing your eye down towards the valley and you will see the Cleddau meandering here and there through the woods into the valley below. Looking southwards you will see a twelve to fifteen-mile stretch of the most beautiful scenery. On the horizon are the woods of Lawrenny, Slebech, Canaston and Landshipping.[8] This is how J Absalom, who lived in these parts some eighty years ago, described the view from the hill overlooking Rhydwilym, the cradle of the Baptist cause for the three ancient counties of Cardiganshire, Carmarthenshire and Pembrokeshire. The Forest of Narberth that once existed had long gone.

The first trees were cut down long before the Christian era. There is some evidence to suspect an Iron Age settlement among the ruins on the site of Narberth Castle. The mythical tales of the Mabinogion speak of Arberth as being a centre for Pwyll, Prince of Dyfed, who held court or *llys*. The actual site is unknown but the present site of the castle is a strong contender: [9] *Within a strong palisade would have been a group of timber buildings the focus of which was the hall, oblong in plan, with six posts to support the roof.*[10] A small clearing was made then at the bottom end of the town, towards Templeton.

As it was the practice of the Welsh fighters to use the woods in which to hide and launch their unsuspecting attacks with their guerrilla warfare tactics, each generation and invader had cut further into the forests and woodland. When the Normans came, so came the woodcutters, as each Norman army would be made up of hundreds of woodcutters and charcoal burners. Also, more timber was needed for weapons and for the line of forts that was erected across what is now known as the Landsker Line, pushing the Welsh towards the poorer soil of the North.

By 1102 Henry I had given rights to the burgesses to cut green timber (for house building) from the Narberth forest and much wood was needed for the Castle. We do not know the exact date for the establishment of this Castle or what the original design looked like but it was most probably a Motte and Bailey structure. We do know, however, that on several occasions it was set on fire due to Welsh uprisings. Gruffydd ap Rhys was said to have burned the Castle near Arberth in 1116. In 1215 the Castle was burned again, this time by the Prince of Gwynedd, Llywelyn ap Iorwerth. He destroyed the Castle once again in 1218 after it had been rebuilt. It was burned yet again, indicating that it was still predominantly made of timber, when Llywelyn ap Gruffudd's forces attacked the Castle in 1257.

By 1378, tenants of Narberth had the right to cut green timber, pick dead wood for fuel and to pasture swine. Real deforestation took apace with the burning in the 14th and 15th century for the use of lead mining. By the mid 16th century the tenants were allowed to cut firewood and timber for fencing at Christmas. It has been claimed that the forest provided timber for the Royal Navy.[11] In 1601-2 seven men were accused of felling no fewer than 1400 oak trees for their own use. In the reign of James I, a survey of the forest between Narberth and Minwear indicated that it contained 3,000 large trees, an extra 11,000 suitable for firewood, and 21,000 saplings.

The coming of the Normans and the felling of the trees symbolised to those around the cutting down of the old order, the old way of life, even the old faith. The Norman invasion of England in 1066 had major repercussions for the Church in Wales, the Diocese of St David's and the inhabitants of Narberth. William the Conqueror came with the Papal blessing, resulting in the subjection of Welsh princedoms and gradually bringing the Welsh Church under the Crown and Government of Canterbury. During this period the presence of the Knights Templar, a military and missionary organization founded by Bernard de Clairvaux, was established in the area and made their base near Narberth, which is now known by the name of Templeton.

By 1284, all the independent Welsh princedoms were completely under Sovereign rule. The Celtic Church, for five centuries, remained mostly unaffected by the Augustine mission and resisted pressure to centralise the Church under Rome's authority. Although it had remained and developed independently it had lost some of the zeal and devotion of the earlier great Saints but it was still the Church of the people, of the Welsh tongue, simple in its worship and not corrupted by the many abuses of the hierarchical political system. But now change was afoot. As Norman castles and church buildings were erected in the land, so the Welsh Celtic Church became subject to Rome.

It is believed that St Andrew's Church (Narberth parish church) was first built by Sir Andrew Perrot,[12] during the early part of the 13th Century.

It was not the big impressive structure we see today, but comprised a Nave, a South Chapel and a Tower. In 1291 Pope Nicholas commanded tithes from its parishioners. The first recorded Rector is Hugh ap Griffin in 1332. The Norman Kings, particularly Henry I, tried to ensure that Bishops appointed to these dioceses were either Normans or others chosen for their allegiance to Norman rule. Due to absenteeism there was a lack of priests and nepotism was widespread, Narberth did not escape its detrimental effect. [13]

The spiritual impact of this policy was disastrous for Wales. True shepherds and spiritual leaders were lost. The Old Celtic Church spoke the native language of the people but the language of the Established Church was Latin and with it a whole superstitious religion developed which knew little of the Good News. With only small congregations attending, buildings became derelict and an example of this spiritual blindness comes from the personal account of Giraldus Cambrensis, who uniquely gives us an understanding of people and places of Wales in the 12th century. When preaching in Haverfordwest, on his travels around Wales recruiting Welsh men for the Crusades in 1188, Gerald preached eloquently. As he said himself *many found it odd and some indeed miraculous that I, the archdeacon, preached the Word of God, speaking first in Latin and in French and those who could not understand a word of either language were just as much moved with tears as the others.* [14] If faith comes by hearing the Word of God, as the Scripture says, you would have thought it needed to be in one's own language. It was superstition rather than faith. This period of history is not known as the Dark Ages without reason, and darkness spread to this corner of Wales.

If there was a glimmer of light for the Gospel during this dark period in this land of Wales then, incredibly, it was to be found here in Pembrokeshire, including Narberth. Rev Albert William Barrah argues in his thesis on *The History of the Reformed Faith in Pembrokeshire,* that Pembrokeshire is not Anglo-Saxon but Anglo-Flemish, being colonised by the Flemish people from 1108 on the authority of Henry I. One social study conducted in the 1970's asked the question of those living in Pembrokeshire if they considered themselves to be Welsh or English. A significant number replied *Neither, I am Pembrokeshire.* Barrah makes the connection between Flemish influence and that of East Anglia, from where Oliver Cromwell hailed. Pembrokeshire alone out of the twelve shires of Wales supported the Parliamentary cause and both the Commander-in-Chief and Adjutant General of the Parliamentary Army came from Pembroke. The reason for this fertile ground of dissent is the connection with the Flemish influence. Remains of the Flemish presence can still be seen in Narberth today. For example, looking up from Market Street towards the War Memorial you will see the HSBC Bank, and to its right is one of the oldest remaining dwellings in Narberth. In the corner of the building you will see evidence of Flemish architecture. The Market Street dwellings apparently existed from 1257. Some were built to house the Flemish soldiers with whom the garrison was strengthened.[15]

In our land we can say that the 11th and 12th centuries were generally apathetic towards religion but Flanders was different. A priest in Flanders by the name of Lambert le Begue, who died in 1187, had a powerful ministry of reform, akin to the flavour of the old Saints of the Celtic Church, where many were converted to a more simple and pure form of the Christian faith, being more in line with the New Testament Church. And it was to Flanders that John Wycliffe (1330-84), who became known as the Morning Star of the Reformation was sent as a Church envoy. On his return he sent out preachers who travelled throughout the country speaking the Gospel as they went and were given the name *Lollard.* This term *Lollard* certainly became known in these parts because it is a Flemish word meaning to *mutter.*

It is uncertain, however, if the Welsh sympathiser, Walter Brut, who followed the principles of Wycliffe and preached along the Welsh border counties, came to Pembrokeshire. He described himself as a sinner, layman, farmer, Christian, and a Welshman who also expressed protestant views.[16] He taught that the Word of God, and not the Pope, should govern Church life. It was in Antwerp that the great Bible translator, William Tyndale, made his base when translating the scriptures into English, although this may not have had much influence on the Welsh-speaking inhabitants as the Bibles were smuggled into the Flemish ports such as Tenby. The Gospel light, although dim, was seen in these parts.

In 1282 Archbishop Peckham conducted a survey throughout England and Wales and was far from happy. He said *the laity lived their lives largely without practical recourse to God. But he was even unhappier with the clergy. Among their more prominent weaknesses, in his view, were drunkenness, cohabitation with women and ignorance.* Indeed, he declared that he had *never come across clergy as illiterate as those found in Wales!*

Another setback for the Welsh clergy was their doomed support of the Owain Glyndwr rebellion. Many of them did, and it was to have adverse repercussions for the Welsh Church. After its failure no Welsh clergy were promoted to high office. Wales became the dioceses of 'poor livings' – where power, prestige and prosperity were so often in short supply. Wales was not the place to be. Many parishes, therefore, became vacant.

The early years of the 16th century saw a time of great change politically and religiously. When Henry VIII established the Anglican Church, the Acts of Union of 1536 and 1539 brought some Reformation to the Church. Scripture was to be the basis of Church teaching. The Bible was translated into English, images were removed and the Communion Table was introduced. All this had little effect in many parts of Wales because of the Welsh language and the people understood neither Latin nor English. It was not until the New Testament and the Book of Common Prayer appeared in Welsh in 1567, and the Welsh Bible in 1588, that improvement came for the indigenous people in their spiritual lives. In Pembrokeshire, where there were the seaports and also where English was spoken, Narberth was more open to change.

St Andrew's Church at the end of the 19th Century

The forsaken places are many in the midst of the land.
But yet a tenth will be in it, And will return and be for consuming.
As a terebinth tree or as an oak, whose stump remains when it is cut down.
So the Holy Seed shall be its stump.

Isaiah 6 : 12 - 13

18

A Seed Planted

The folk that went from Narberth to witness the sight of William Nichol burning at the stake in Haverfordwest said they would never forget the stink in their nostrils of human flesh burning. There was something else they never forgot - the testimony of a martyr. As the Word stands, the Church would grow by the blood of the martyrs and three of the four martyrs burned for their faith in Wales came from Pembrokeshire.[17]

Of Robert Ferrar, who was burned in Carmarthen, it is said that his death did leave a very deep impression upon the people of the southwest with his final words to the crowd *if you see me flinch do not accept my doctrine.* Ferrar had been Bishop of St David's but by the time of his execution in 1555 Henry Morgan had replaced him. To be a Protestant during the reign of Mary I was to live a perilous existence, as Protestant sympathies were not to be expressed without danger to one's life. What must it have been like for Rev Lewis Williams 1540-1617 who, as Rector of Narberth, married the daughter of Robert Ferrar after the martyrdom of her father? This surely would not have gone unnoticed by those in authority. Imagine yourself in such a position, a near relative being publicly scorned for having similar beliefs to your own and with every word of your preaching being scrutinised. Instructions given in his final Will reveal his Protestant leanings. [18]

What was it about this area that made it a Protestant hotbed of dissent, more so than other areas of Wales? Well, the diocese of St David's was the scene of the first stage of the Protestant offensive in Wales. William Barlow, the first Prior at Haverfordwest and then Bishop from 1536, was committed to the faith of the Protestant cause, showing that a person is saved by faith alone in Jesus Christ, apart from any religious act of piety. Barlow was determined to establish wholehearted Protestantism in the Diocese. In 1534, whilst Prior of Haverfordwest, he opened his campaign with a series of anti-papal sermons and went on the attack by claiming that no-one preached God's Word, and that very few were in favour of it. Immorality and idolatry were common in the Diocese, which he supposed was corrupt, but none so far removed or so extreme as to be without hope of reformation. During the turbulent years of Henry, Edward, Mary and Elizabeth, the doctrinal reforms made little impact on the Welsh Church but, nevertheless, it was enough for the blood of martyrs in this area to be shed.

When John Penry published a pamphlet in 1587 on the spiritual condition of Wales, he described its forlorn desolation in heart-rending expressions. With Elizabeth I on the throne, at least the immediate fear from persecution was not so keenly felt and, slowly, reform and Puritanism became the order of the day. It made inroads to this now rapidly changing community. Narberth was becoming more of a rural centre for commerce. When Leland visited Narberth in 1530, it was called 'a village' but by 1562 it was called 'a town'. There had been a fourfold increase in population in less than a century to reach a total of about 450 inhabitants.

A local Vicar of Amroth by the name of Peregrine Philips, born in 1623, was one who came to embody both Protestant and Puritan views. He became noted for his powers as a preacher with his ability to preach in both English and Welsh. He had a very influential position in the religious life of West Wales and preached at Pembroke Castle at the time Cromwell and his troops besieged it. He became known as the Apostle of Pembrokeshire.

The Parliamentary Army's arrival at Narberth was to have a profound religious effect. It is said that the old parish church of Mounton at Canaston (still part of the parish of St Andrew's) held great prayer meetings whilst troops hid out in the woods. Cromwell's army was a mixture of all sorts of Protestant persuasion. There were Presbyterians, Independents, Baptists, Fifth Monarchists, Quakers and others. We cannot imagine an army made up of men whose interests were the Bible, Doctrine and Church polity. We still have reminders of the Parliament's presence with us even to this day. Plain Dealings is so named after one of Cromwell's Colonels who lived in the cottage on Redstone Road. Providence Hill was so named by Cromwell's army and from which he attacked the castle. Narberth market was first set up by Captain Richard Castle, who played a military role in the Civil War and was rewarded with land at Narberth (he was a dissenter). Robert Tounson was inducted to the living of Narberth in 1646 and was licensed, with Peregrine Phillips, for the Propagation of the Gospel in these parts. [19]

We have an indication of how deeply the Puritan faith had taken root when, in 1662, the monarchy was restored and the counter reforms of Archbishop Laud. Thomas Warren of Narberth publicly informed his parishioners that the Prayer Book was a pack of lies and the invention of men. Richard Cromwell, in 1659, appointed Thomas Warren as a preacher to Narberth. Christopher Jackson, Rector of Llanddewi Velfrey, mixed pages from *the prayer book with tobacco in his pipe and warned all and sundry that only the wicked welcomed the return of the King.* [20] The reformation had left few Roman Catholics in Pembrokeshire and by 1676 Narberth parish contained only one.

After Cromwell's death in 1658 and with the monarchy being restored in 1660, Nonconformists were denied the right to worship in their own way and punishment ranged from a fine of £5 for the first offence to 'transportation' for the third. By 1681, Nonconformity had become a real force in Pembrokeshire. In that year, a large number of dissenters were presented at the Sessions for refusing to attend church services of the Established Church. Some names of interest for us included Richard Castle of Narberth, gent[21]; Griffith Howell of Narberth, yeoman; John Poyer of Robeston, yeoman.

Those were dark days for the Gospel and it was to Rushacre in Narberth, just a quarter of a mile up Redstone Road, that those who wished to worship God with freedom in the Spirit, rather than in a fleshly way, resorted. One name that will always be linked with Narberth is Griffith Howell of Rushacre. He was a man of influence and substance, a Preacher of the Gospel in both English and Welsh. He was one of six people baptised by William Jones, the ejected Vicar of Cilmaenllwyd near Rhydwilym, an able man who could also preach in both languages - not an easy task! Services were held at Rushacre

Farm, which became the location of the first Baptist Church at Narberth, although there was no chapel building. By 1668 the members increased to twenty-one and after two years they numbered sixty. Many suffered imprisonment, loss of possessions and persecution for their faith.

Griffith Howell of Narberth was present at the formation of one of the historic confessions of faith, namely the 1689 Baptist Confession, which is adhered to by Baptists throughout the world to this day. It stands as one of the most erudite, orthodox, balanced, spiritually rich theological treatises ever written. To have had two men from Narberth be involved in this work (William Jones being the other) is a testimony to the rich teaching and great light that must have been in the town at that time.

It is difficult for us now to appreciate the local importance and significance of Rushacre for the Baptist cause in this area. Between 1660-88 the Baptists in Carmarthen town disappeared and other Baptists were scattered. At this desperate time Rushacre became one of the most important places for Baptists in the whole of Carmarthenshire, Pembrokeshire and Cardiganshire, occupying a position of supreme significance. When the Baptist cause was collapsing, Rushacre saw one hundred and thirteen conversions.[22] The members were mostly from the poor, rural classes and dispersed throughout as many as 38 parishes, mostly in Pembrokeshire but also including some from Carmarthenshire and Cardiganshire.

William Jones was arrested one day whilst preaching at Rushacre and placed in Haverfordwest prison. Like William Jones, Griffith Howell, over a forty-year period, spent more periods in jail for his faithful preaching than anyone else, with the possible exception of the Quakers. No sect was imbued with a stronger sectarian consciousness than the Baptists. With their views on *believer's baptism* as opposed to infant baptism, the non-Baptist dissenters and Established Church stood shoulder-to-shoulder in opposition to Baptist teaching, believing it to be a revolutionary rite fraught with peril. They considered Baptists as social incendiaries and saw them as a threat to political stability and social authority. The Independents did not want to be tarred with the same brush of extremism.

Rev W H Williams, Minister of Hill Park Baptist Church, Haverfordwest, in 1931, highlighted the contribution of Griffith Howell to the Baptist cause and to him belongs the honour of not only providing the first meeting place but also the resting place for the dead. Nonconformists were not only hated in life but also refused a decent burial in death. Some were buried in their gardens. It was not until 1886 that the law was changed to allow Nonconformists burial in consecrated ground. The burial place at Trefangor became the equivalent of Westminster Abbey for the Baptists of the county. The first one to be buried there was Griffith's son, John. The freedom we have to worship today did not just happen; it came from the determination of such men. It was, however, another 150 years before a Baptist Church was finally formed in Narberth.

The kingdom of heaven is like a mustard seed, which a man took and
sowed in his field, which indeed is the least of all the seeds: but when
it is grown it is greater than the herbs and becomes a tree, so that the birds
of the air come and nest in its branches.

Matthew 13 : 31

William Nichol Memorial, High Street, Haverfordwest

Fire in the Forest

As the town expanded it drew people of various Christian persuasions, both orthodox and unorthodox. What goes around also comes to Narberth! By 1670, in less than a century, there had been a significant increase in population. Narberth had become a commercial centre, with the starting of a weekly market by Captain Richard Castle during the Commonwealth. One of the factors in the 57% rise of population in Narberth, compared to the preceding century, was the need for labourers in the local economy, which was based on coal mining and limestone quarries.[23] Men came from the north in the summertime to quarry lime towards the south of the town. To the north, the character of the land was of a rich red hue, hence the name Redstone Road. This land was fertile and well cultivated.

Narberth became more diverse than most rural towns and villages in this area, with newcomers looking for work and setting up businesses. They brought with them knowledge and ideas from a wider world. Narberth became an exchange for both local and national news and it was a centre-point and stopping place for travellers. It is interesting to note that the Royal Mail route ran from London through Narberth. In 1748, twelve people were licensed to keep what were called *alehouses* in Narberth. By 1813 there were eighteen public houses in the town and by 1826 the number had increased to twenty-four. Farmers would travel from the surrounding district to sell their cattle and other animals at the monthly fairs in the town. There was plenty of business, therefore, for the alehouses. [24]

Between 1670 and 1801 the population of Narberth parish trebled, with new streets, buildings, businesses, banks, a courthouse and pavements added to the town. It is said that Narberth was the first town in South Wales to have electric lighting but how true this is, is hard to determine as many towns make the same claim. However, we do know that Narberth had become a local centre, not just in commercial terms but also for Christians of all persuasions.

From the 17th century Narberth became a haven for the Baptists of the three counties and a bastion for the cause at a perilous time in history. But it was not only the Baptists who had come to the town, because other dissenters also met here. The Quakers diverged from traditional Christianity and Catholicism with their focus now on the *Inner light.* The Quakers gathered illegally in private houses, as meeting in the open-air was a great risk; yet in this area they had a large following. After the death of Cromwell, not one day passed in a thirty-year period without the presence of a Quaker being in prison at Haverfordwest.[25] Two from Narberth who suffered were John Husband and Evan Protheroe. In 1700 they built a small meetinghouse on the east side of the road from Narberth to Redstone, the oldest such meetinghouse in Wales. The site is believed to be at Blaenmarlais. Richard Davies, who was a Quaker preacher, gives us an account of his coming to meet with Quaker friends at Narberth. *I came to the house of our friend Lewis Davies [David of Llanddewi Velfrey]. Staying there some time they lent me a horse to go to a meeting at Redstone [about a mile from Narberth Castle]... when I came to the place the meeting was out of doors, there being no house that I knew that could contain the multitude of people.* He goes on to describe the meeting but as he was coming out two soldiers, who were the sons of a priest, had come with guns to arrest him but they had no official warrant so he withstood them.

In 1662 William Penn visited America and returned with enthusiasm for establishing a colony there for the Friends. Many from Pembrokeshire warmed to the idea, one of the first being Lewis Davis from Llanddewi Velfrey, who bought 3,000 acres for £60.[26] From Narberth went John Scourfield, gentleman, son and heir of Maurice Scourfield, and also a number from Redstone, namely Thomas Ellis, 1663, Francis Jones, 1711, Daniel Lewis, Gentleman, 1682. It is uncertain how many went from this area but the name of Narberth in Pennsylvania suggests the strength of a Quaker connection with this town. Interestingly, 150 years later Benjamin Thomas received a call to a Baptist Church in the States and also, when Myfyr Emlyn lectured in the USA, it was to Pennsylvania he went. The Quakers still meet in Narberth today, although their original place of worship ceased to be used from 1776.

Shortly after building the Quaker house, a fire started in the religious life of this land not far from Narberth. John Phillips and John Vaughan were instrumental along with Griffith Jones, through the work of the SPCK, in providing Christian education for the people of Wales. Years before, John Wesley would say *his heart was strangely warmed*, and this could be said to be the beginning of the Methodist Revival.

Before Methodism, Griffith Jones was at work in Llanddowror near St Clears. The fire was felt when God took hold of him in 1715 and thousands went to hear him preach. All the Welsh Revivalists made their way to this small village. Being on the main road to Carmarthen, there were those from Narberth too who would have heard this Word as they passed along the way.

As he recorded in his journal, it was the road that the preacher Caleb Morris of Tabernacle took many times. Daniel Rowland, considered by many the greatest preacher of all, was converted under Griffith Jones' ministry. Howel Harris went to him for advice and became a teacher in the Circulating Schools of Wales. It is estimated that 300,000 Welsh people were taught to read through these schools. William Morgan's Bible was the textbook. Harris, the great exhorter of the Methodist cause, taught in this town [27] and Williams Williams' (Pantycelyn) wife lived for a time in the home of Griffith Jones. Williams Pantycelyn, the great Welsh hymn writer, who wrote *Guide me O thou Great Jehovah, pilgrim through this barren land*, preached in the parish church of Mounton, where Cromwell's army had met a century before. Howell Davies served as his Curate.

Through the ranks of the Calvinistic Methodist movement in Pembrokeshire at this time, the Rev Howell Davies earned the title of The Apostle of Pembrokeshire. Although not much is known of his early life, he first appears at the school of Griffith Jones, Llanddowror. *He was Griffith Jones' favourite pupil, and on the day of his ordination the venerable clergyman appealed to the congregation at Llanddowror to raise their prayers to heaven on his behalf.* [28]

His connection with the parish of Narberth came when he became Curate at Llys-y-fran. He began his ministry at the beginning of the year 1740 and proceeded at once to thunder forth against the ungodliness of the region with such vigour that the local ne'er-do-wells trembled at his presence.[29] Although only at Llys-y-fran for eight months, Howell Davies also preached and administered the sacraments at St Daniel in Castlemartin and at Mounton near Narberth, both places being in the English region of the county. The sum of his communicants in all three churches was over two thousand. The buildings would be filled and emptied two or three times on Communion Sundays, such were the numbers of applicants eagerly desiring to commemorate the death of the cross. [30]

Howell Davies was predominantly the apostle of Pembrokeshire. His apostleship was directed as fully towards the English–speaking area of the county as towards the Welsh. But his labours were not confined only to Pembrokeshire. William Williams in his elegy of him referred to the extent of the labours:

> They tell us how he journeyed,
> When his health was still preserved,
> When Monmouth, Denbigh, Gwynedd,
> Merioneth, Flint, he served;
> How he proclaimed the gospel,
> In his fluent, lively way,
> From Presteigne to St David's
> Holyhead to Cardiff bay. [31]

Howell Davies was a most powerful preacher. The older believers accounted him second only to Daniel Rowland himself. He would read his text clearly, he spoke slowly to begin with but soon it was sensed that his soul was stirred within him. He would raise his voice like a trumpet and the congregation would stand confounded before him. He would hurl the severest darts at his hearers and every sentence would wound. Hundreds would groan and sigh. Tears would be flowing freely and there would not be one dry cheek in the crowd.[32] William Williams calls him 'the shepherd of four large churches, these were Capel Newydd; Woodstock; St Daniel, Castlemartin and Mounton, Narberth.

The legacy of the preaching of these men, Howell Harries and Howell Davies was Nebo Calvinistic Methodist Church, which in 1843 became part of the strongest of all the denominational Churches in Wales, yet struggled for many years until its closure (now Chapel Field Gardens in Narberth).

It was George Whitefield who first spurred on John Wesley to preach in the open air, and many have considered Whitefield not only as the better preacher of the two but one of the greatest preachers in the history of the Christian Church. Thousands came to hear him preach and so it was when he came to Narberth to preach on 17th April 1743. *I went that evening to Narberth and I preached to some thousands with great power they were not unlike the colliers of Kingswood. He writes again in his diary on 20th April, I preached yesterday at eight in the morning to about eight thousand people in that place, (Haverfordwest) and in the afternoon to several thousands at Narberth, both times with great power.* [33] Although we do not know the text on which Whitefield preached, someone once asked him "why do you always preach, *you must be born again?"* his simple answer was because YOU MUST!

On Monday 7th May 1781, John Wesley preached near the market place where *an abundance of people flocked together.* He noted that *they were still as night.* [34] It was during his travels into Pembrokeshire that Wesley became more convinced than ever that preaching like an apostle without joining together those who were awakened and training them in the ways of God is only *begetting children for the murderer. How much preaching has there been for these twenty years all over Pembrokeshire? But no regular societies, no discipline, no order.* For Wesley, people were in a worse condition due to the fact there was little discipleship. A Methodist Society was formed in 1796 and a chapel built in 1811 on the site of the present library.

Another great preacher who visited these parts was Christmas Evans, 1781-1840, also known as 'The one-eyed preacher of Wales'. He preached in the Baptist Association held at Ffynnon and the crowds gathered in their thousands. He preached powerfully on Hebrews 5:9, *Christ the Prince of our Salvation.* The apocryphal account of that day mentioned *it was a hot day and the wagons from the brewery were driven out to supply the required refreshments. The Baptists drank the town dry!*

We have noted that the Quakers found a place here in Narberth during the 18th Century but so did other groups. The Moravian Movement, led by John Gambold, launched its cause in Pembrokeshire with an orthodox branch of Protestantism that followed a communal pattern of living for evangelistic, mission-minded people having a desire for true piety, radical in the application of the commands of Christ to one's life. Its main settlement was in Haverfordwest, with four preaching stations in the county, one being at Narberth in 1765. During this century, Narberth would have been a hotbed for theological discussion. Along with fervent religion can also come false fire and the fire that sometimes burned at Narberth in those days was not necessarily fire from above. So often the persecuted become the persecutors as one group fell out with the other.

Fire literally did fall in the year 1796, on 26th of January at about three thirty in the afternoon. *There happened in and around the town a severe tempest of thunder and lightning attended with rain and hail stones. The lightning split asunder the steeple, dismantling the bells and shivering their frames to pieces. The lightning first struck the iron work of the weather clock, descended the tower and exploded in the body of the church and carrying away every pane of glass in the windows and demolishing every pew in the chancel, melting the nails in them.*[35] In the eyes of the dissenters this was a great work of the Lord.

The Established Church was active in curtailing the spread and influence of Nonconformity and the Nonconformists were not without sin against the new Methodist movement. The concern of the Anglican Church was the threat against the spiritual authority of the Bishop and Priest, whereas the "experience meetings" of Calvinistic Methodists[36] become the main means of Grace for the believers' spiritual growth. For the Puritan Nonconformists, the concern that led to opposition of the Methodists had to do with some emotional excess and in some cases the doctrinal uncertainty of some of its advocates. In Narberth this was not without warrant.

John Relly (1712-1778), who was from Jefferson, became a convert and follower of the Methodist movement. He preached on many occasions for the revivalist George Whitefield at his Tabernacle Chapel in London but deviated later from the faith. He was excommunicated from Welsh Calvinistic Methodism and then crossed swords with John Wesley in 1756 on the issue of the Salvation that Christ has provided. By this time, Relly had gathered his own following, called the Pembrokeshire Universalists, and on his first tour in 1741 he established a place of worship at Rhyddlangwraig, [37] near Narberth, which existed until 1815. Just like the Quakers, they did not practice baptism in any form and believed that as Christ died for all, even those who did not come to believe in Him or those who rejected Him, would still be saved. He spread his beliefs to America and is acknowledged as one of the pre-founders of the Unitarian movement.

At the beginning of the 19th century the Preseli hills were on fire with revival religion as the farmers made their way to the cattle fairs and as the locals came to market to trade and collect their mail. They brought with them a fervour and zeal that was to run throughout the mountains, hills and valleys of this county. During the previous hundred years in Wales, dissenters were known as *dry dissenters* and not without cause. The Methodist movement embodied life but without the freedom to express their faith in the Established Church. It was not until 1811 that the Welsh Calvinistic Methodists became a separate denomination. Fire was to burn now in the Denominational Churches of the Baptists, Congregationalists and Independents. Narberth was to have its own blazing fire.

In 1934 R T Jenkins wrote *"why was Pembrokeshire and its borders so liable as Athens of old to welcome "new religions"? Everyone had a go – not only the Independents and Particular Baptists and the two Methodist connexions but Unitarians, General Baptists, Moravians, Huntingtonians, Sandemanians, Rellites and even the Muggletonians?"*

A view of the old Flemish building
from Market Square

NARBERTH.
Pembrokeshire.

Do we not have a God to please, a soul to save, an account to give, heaven to seek, hell to flee from? Is not religion the most beneficial and advantageous, and also the most joyful and desirable thing in the whole world?

Griffith Jones

Two Large Trees

Many branches of the Christian Church sprouted up in what became fertile soil in Narberth. The ground of people's hearts had been ploughed, stones removed and seeds planted. The prayers of the faithful, who longed for and had hope, that the good news would take root, watered the seed. Many causes sprouted only for a moment then to wither away. Two places of worship took root and grew to become a great influence for the cause of Christ within the town, neighbourhood and to the ends of the earth. These two Churches became known as Bethesda Baptist and Tabernacle Congregational Church.

From the Minister's room of Bethesda, two large sycamore trees are visible from the window and symbolise to me the stories and history of these two Churches. Both of these sycamore trees were planted about the same time, about 200 years ago, one slightly younger than the other. Both took root and grew together, both were watered with the same rain, both grew strong through the same wind that blew across Plas Farm and both began to decline with similar diseases and with their roots being inextricably intertwined. This is the story of Bethesda and Tabernacle. Both constituted in the same year, both grew rapidly during the early years, both had ministers of exceptional abilities, both were founded on Biblical teaching, both were Calvinistic in doctrine, teaching Salvation through Jesus Christ by faith in Him alone. Both suffered under the rebuttal of the Established Church for being Nonconformists, both were blessed with the out-pouring of the Spirit of God that took place over a 50 year period in Pembrokeshire, and both succumbed to the downgrading and undermining of Biblical religion.

Bethesda Baptist Church

This 19th century was the golden age of Nonconformity. The dramatic growth of the Baptist and Nonconformist causes in this area reflected what was happening throughout the land. By the second half of the nineteenth century, one third of the people of Pembrokeshire were Baptists. A Baptist witness had been in Narberth for 150 years before the six members who worshipped at Molleston and lived in Narberth between 1730-31 formed Bethesda Baptist Church. The Welsh speaking Baptists from Narberth worshipped at Ffynnon. It was not until 1808 that a few devoted believers felt the time had now arrived for a Baptist cause to be established in Narberth itself. A co-pastor of Molleston Church, named Rev William Thomas, lived in the Narberth High Street. He had a great zeal for the Gospel and erected the first meeting place for Bethesda whilst carrying on a business, so as to avoid being dependent on the ministry for support. He set apart a building behind his residence on a 999-year lease, at a nominal rent of 5 shillings per year. The first services were held on Sunday afternoons and on weekday evenings, and this cause was part of Molleston until 1816.

The Church was formed as a Particular Baptist Cause, adhering to the Baptist Confession of Faith, 1689, to which Griffith Howell and William Jones had put their names 150 years previously. Believing such truths as the inability of man to come to God in his own strength, the unconditional love of God, that Christ died for a particular people - those who would come to faith in Him. They believed in the irresistible Grace of God in bringing people to Himself, and the perseverance of the Saints in the Christian faith of this Church. Every Minister called was to adhere to these beliefs. In the deeds of the Church it says, that the meetinghouse was for the purpose of congregating to *pray, read and hear the Scriptures of God's Holy Word read, preached and expounded, and to administer the ordinance of baptism and the Lord's Table.* [38]

The new Church consisted of forty two members, comprising twenty four transferred from Molleston, three from Ffynnon, nine from Haverfordwest, three from Beulah, two from Ebenezer and one from Cardigan. By 1817 the Church was in a position to maintain its own Pastor and the growth was remarkable. In just one year, from 1816 – 17, the congregation doubled from 42 to 84 members and more were to come. John Morgan of Newcastle Emlyn was the first Minister to be called, in April 1817. He was a man of commanding appearance, high culture and a very popular preacher. In five years he had received 72 people into membership of the Church. The next was another able preacher called Benjamin Thomas, whose home church was Salem, Meidrim, which was formed in 1769. Meidrim was the place where puritan Stephen Hughes translated many protestant tracts and religious works into the Welsh language. It is hard to overstate the importance of this man's work and distribution of religious works without which there would have been no Nonconformist revival. There is a story that in the time of Benjamin Thomas, the local Vicar of Meidrim parish took to firing his gun at the Baptist worshippers as they made their way to Salem, down the hill from the Church. In such days, to worship at a Nonconformist chapel was an act of real conviction.

Benjamin was a student at the Baptist College in Bradford but how he came to be known by the Church is not certain. We do know, however, that he resided at Whitley Farm during the closing years of his life, which was owned at one time by a Daniel Thomas, whose name is written on the deeds of the Church and who was also instrumental in the purchasing of the land. Bradford College was by no means a purely academic training college; it also placed an emphasis on evangelism. Benjamin was invited to the Church to supply the pulpit on a three-month probation period, not a dissimilar procedure to my own - it is a step of faith for a Church when calling a man straight from college. His ministry was to be a lifetime's work and much blessed of the Lord in establishing the Baptist cause in the town. He served the Church from October 1822 to July 1st 1862. It was a long, powerful and successful ministry and even 30 years after his death his name was frequently upon the lips and in the memory of the town's people.

After fifteen years, the chapel building became too small for the congregation. Despite having extended the original building and adding a gallery, a new place of worship was still needed. In 1837, J H Allen, Esq; Cresselly, offered the Church one of the best sites in the middle of the town, with two cottages and with a place for burial, for a sum of £600. The old building was torn down and the materials used for the new. The cast iron pillars, which are currently downstairs in Bethesda's schoolroom, are remains from the chapel built at that time. For some reason, a baptistery was not built and Baptisms took place at Coxlake, adjoining the turnpike road leading to Robeston Wathen. In November 1837, the chapel opened with a membership of 250 and a Sunday school of 170.

However, the Baptist cause was under great financial pressure, between the purchase and building costs, and soon had to sell one of the cottages for £400. By 1854 Benjamin Thomas' health had begun to fail and he was served to the end of his ministry by two assistants. [39] The plaque inside the chapel captures the nature and period of ministry with the words *thou wast faithful in the strife; he shall receive the crown of life*. Benjamin knew suffering, having had a son who died in infancy but he also had another son who followed him into the ministry and whom he named after himself. If we assume, *like father like son*, and that he was *a chip off the old block*, we have a flavour of the radical nature of Benjamin Thomas here in Narberth, from the preaching of his son who became known as "Thomas of Toronto". He left a series of sermons from his pulpit at Jarvis Street.

By the 1920's, Jarvis Street had a very distinctive witness, contending for the Reformed faith in Canada with a magazine called *The Gospel Witness* and also with a college to train men for the ministry. Dr T T Shields, who was Pastor of Jarvis Church, would say *Dr Thomas was one of the most glorious souls I have ever met, and absolutely true to the Word of God.* "Thomas of Toronto" came back and preached many times in this pulpit of Bethesda. His name is recorded in the Encyclopaedia of Canadian Biography; *Born near Narberth, Pembrokeshire on the 23rd of January 1843. He comes of a good stock.* The title from of one of his sermons, taken from Romans 6:8-11, gives the idea of the Christ-centred nature of his message *The one Christ the only Christ; the one atonement and only atonement; the one death the perennial life.* [40] Glorious truths that are Christ-centred.

One illuminating account of the strength of Nonconformity in the town during the ministry of Benjamin Thomas was the march of 1000 people to the ancient Baptist burial ground at Trefangor, a plot of about 33 square feet lying on the left side of the main road going to Ffynnon chapel. It was a piece of ground purchased by Griffith Howell of Rushacre who provided not only the first meeting place for the Baptists but also the last resting place for the dead. On 13th June 1684, the 20th year of the reign of Charles II, Griffith Jones acquired this parcel of ground for the burying of the Baptist dead. It is hard to describe the extent of feelings this issue of burial raised for Baptists and other Nonconformists alike. They held to the orthodox belief of the resurrection of the body. All who are in the graves will hear the voice of the Son of God and we will be called to give an account before the Judgement Seat in the body.

In 1861 an incident occurred with the death of David Griffith, Accrington, which was to stir this peaceful resting place: David Griffith was a distinguished Baptist preacher who was born in the parish of Trefelyn, Pembrokeshire. He had studied at Ffynnon with the purpose of going into the ministry. Often, when at the academy, he would draw aside to this peaceful spot and express his wish to be buried there. When David Griffith died, a grave was dug and the coffin carrying the mortal remains was brought from Lancashire. Many travelled 200 miles to attend his funeral.

When they arrived they were told that Mr J Lewis of Henllan, a local gentleman who had bought Trefangor Farm which surrounded the little burial plot, would not allow any funeral to take place unless a fee was paid to him as recognition of his legal right to it. However, the Baptist leaders would not surrender. They buried the body temporarily in Bethesda's graveyard on October 26th 1861. This was not the end of the matter. Leading Baptist men met to discuss the matters in hand and on November the 4th 1861 an exceptional event took place. David Griffith had a second funeral and this was to be far more demonstrative than the first. Crowds of people made their way to Narberth in defence of the right of their denomination. Rev B Thomas arranged the service at the chapel before proceeding with the coffin of David Griffith to Trefangor. There were estimated to be thousands of people present and the excitement was intense. On their arrival, Mr Lewis of Henllan was waiting, not to receive, but to reject them. Thorns and other bushes had been placed on the road leading to the cemetery in order to obstruct their path. Mr Rees, acting solicitor from Haverfordwest and an unflinching member of the denomination, called on Mr Lewis to have these removed, however, he refused. Several in the procession cleared them away but on reaching the gate they found that it was locked. Mr Lewis was requested to open the gate or give the key. On his declining to do either, Mr Rees took a hammer and broke the gate lock open and the funeral proceeded to the Cemetery. Men with spades and pickaxes set to work to re-open the grave, during which time the various ministers addressed the people.

After Benjamin Thomas, a promising student and another powerful preacher was called, his name was John Williams. He remained only five years, until 1862. He was a great social reformer and raised the moral tone of the town by a considerable degree. Social reform was high on the Baptist agenda and in 1833 a number of members of Bethesda, together with some from Tabernacle, lobbied parliament for the emancipation of slaves.

By the 1880's Narberth had a reputation as a hard-drinking town. The Birmingham Post reported that *there was one public house to every score of persons!* There were twenty-five in all and twenty-three of these were kept by members and deacons of the Baptist and Independent Churches. This article provoked outrage in the town as the Temperance Movement had a strong hold at this time, particularly among the Nonconformists. In their response, it was found that eight of the publicans were Baptists and five were Independents, none of them deacons; and the other twelve were churchgoers. [41]

A closing description, given by a visitor to the chapel sometime in the spring of 1884, invokes the welfare of the cause. The Rev T Evans of Molleston had been preaching during the evening service and the sacred edifice was filled with attentive hearers. After the preaching, eight young men who attended the Sunday School were baptised. *The church is in a most flourishing condition, the saints are edified, our enemies are cowed.*[42]

The Sanctuary

Tabernacle Congregational Church

Although the Baptist cause was started in Narberth in 1808, it was recognised as a branch of Molleston until 1816. Was it denominational rivalry that spurred others to constitute themselves as a Church by forming the Congregational Church? Tabernacle came into being in 1816, with twelve members. A number of these came from the famous Henllan Congregation, about eight miles away and others from Carven. By 1817 there were twenty nine members and when they called Mr W H Lewis in 1818 there were fifty nine members, in 1822 sixty six members, in 1824 eighty members and by 1874 there were two hundred and fifty four members. The highest recorded membership was in 1887 with three hundred and eight members but after seven years this had gone down to two hundred and eighteen. The reason for this one-third decline is not known. The history of this Church followed, as mentioned, the same course as Bethesda but the one difference between the two causes was that the Ministers of Bethesda had long ministries whilst Tabernacle had thirteen Ministers in the first hundred years.

Tabernacle Chapel was opened in 1818, perhaps with the ordination of their first Minister Mr W H Lewis, a student from Carmarthen, for the occasion. The Evangelical Magazine 1819 states, *the hand of providence has been visible in the building of the chapel, the formation of the church and the settlement of the Minister. The lively hopes...and the earnest and generous spirit manifested by one individual...to bear all cost of the building.* Mr Lewis wrote a fine biography in praise of the Principal of the Carmarthen Academy the Rev D Peter, a truly great man, who preached at the ordination service on *The Duty of the Minister*. The second sermon given on the day was by the Rev Morgan Jones, Trelech, on *The Duty of the Church.* Tabernacle was a committed Church with prayer meetings on Sunday mornings at seven o' clock. It is said that prayer is the powerhouse of the Church and this Church was born in prayer and continued in prayer. There was a spiritual temperature about the work. In 1895 there was an Association Meeting held at Tabernacle on spiritual progress, with a fine sermon on *The Need of Prayer in the Work* and *Cause of Christ* by John Phillips.

With the call of Tabernacle's second Minister, Caleb Morris, the Church rapidly grew. His gifts attracted attention both near and far. Although only staying for four years, until 1827, he was still fondly remembered with tales of his ministry being recorded up to the 1860's. In 1828 the Rev Henry Davies became the longest serving Minister of Tabernacle. In these nineteen years the Church grew during his whole term of ministry; his was a steady work. Henry Davies founded a seminary in which he trained a number of young men for the ministry. It was during the next ministry, of Joseph Morris, who was ordained at Tabernacle in October 1849 that the present building was opened on October 4th 1858. The purchase price and building was around £1,000 (the equivalent of £73,000 in today's money). One considers the commitment of the people involved who made pledges of £550 pounds, and during the opening services a collection of £220 (£16,000 in today's value) was taken. The church was declared free from debt at the close of the service.

Tabernacle called another preacher who was to become a prominent leader of the Congregational cause, Joseph Morris. Then there was another, John Morlais Jones, who was a man of the truth and it is said he was loyal to the truth at all costs. Sermons preached by him are recorded in *Cup of Cold Water*.[43] He was full of profound evangelical thought and feeling. The people of Narberth knew the Gospel going forth with power and clarity for many years.

The Gospel always raises, at every level, the welfare of any community. Starting in the home and spreading into all the main societies of the town – with the establishing of educational development for the young and the care and nursing of the elderly and sick - a religious culture was established in Wales. The welfare of the poor and the running of social matters were led by those from the chapels and church of the town. A literary and scientific institution existed with seventy-six members in 1854 and with a library of 162 volumes housed in Market Street. Hugh Cunningham, the Rector, who died in 1714, left the interest on £20 for a master to teach poor children in the parish. Griffith Jones provided three months instruction for children and adults in Bible reading and catechism, during the year 1764 sixty-six pupils attended. In the central aisle of St Andrew's Church, the gravestone of George Devonald of Sodston House records that he charged £30 a year on the farm at Rushacre for an educational charity. This trust appears to have been in operation until probably the 1920's.

Both Bethesda and Tabernacle placed great importance on what was to become the Sunday School Movement. It was mainly the Sunday Schools work which was to become the bedrock for the future of the causes. Tabernacle was the location for the Nonconformist British School and became a Board School in 1871, before it moved to its premises on the Town Moor. The church sought to meet the educational needs of its children with the Intermediate School for those of the Nonconformist constituency in the area. In March 1890 a public meeting was held at Narberth Board School to establish what was to become Narberth Grammar School. The Rev Lewis James of Brynbank, Lampeter Velfrey, laid the foundation stone in September 1895. The continuing influence of the church was felt through its members. John Morgan, a prominent member of Tabernacle, ran a private Grammar School in the town from 1888. He was the first headmaster of the Intermediate School and was appointed at a meeting held in Tabernacle vestry in 1895. He is described as a tall, dignified man with piercing eyes and a prominent Adam's apple, bearing in his features the ravages of ill health, which affected him throughout his life. His pupils held him in great affection and it was said *he did the work of earth in the spirit of heaven.*[44] When Rev W E Stephens was Minister of Bethesda from 1901-37, and was Chairman of the Grammar School, throughout the years he delivered the address on Speech Day.

The fruit seen of the Christian witness was present throughout the community, with its Ministers and Clergy being prominent, not just in the ecclesiastical arena, but also the political and judicial life of the town. The ordinary members of the church community, irrespective of whichever their place of worship, were active and often instigators in establishing many of the societies and organisations that make a community. [45]

Benjamin Thomas (Myfyr Emlyn)

They will be called mighty oaks, a planting of the Lord for the display of his splendour.

Isaiah 61 : 3

Myfyr Emlyn

Probably the opening of Bethesda's new Chapel Building

Great Boughs

By the 1850's the Nonconformist denominations were reaching the zenith of their spiritual life. The 19th century, both locally and nationally, was a time of extraordinary growth. That was not only the result of social factors but also a spiritual awakening to the claims of Christ that gripped the Principality. The Nonconformist pulpit exercised enormous influence for many years in shaping the thinking of the Welsh nation. R S Thomas, in his poem *The Chapel*, describes how a Nonconformist preacher 'caught fire' before his hearers. There was no greater honour in the community than to hold such a position as a *prophet of the Lord*. The picture 'pin-ups' that hung in the homes of the nation were of its preachers and Narberth was not without its 'superstars' who were revered throughout the nation.

A tree is made up of many branches, some small and seemingly insignificant and others great and prominent. Two such boughs were to be found in Narberth. The first grew from the early ministry of Tabernacle. Caleb Morris became its second Minister in 1823, yet he was really second to none. He was born on August 5th 1800, and brought up at the foot of the Preseli hills in Whitchurch, Penygroes. Even as a young boy he passed through deep religious experiences. Like Jacob of old, he wrestled with God. Penygroes was the place where he met with God in prayer and it was at the same place that he learned to preach His name. When only just a boy of fourteen years of age he preached his first sermon where his neighbours came to sympathise and also to criticise the young upstart but, as they listened in astonishment, they realised that a great man was arising in their midst and they sat in admiration. His fame as a preacher soon spread rapidly throughout the country.

The environment played a great part in Caleb's development. Whitchurch was, and still is in many ways, a rural community cut off from much of the English influence that had penetrated the low Pembrokeshire land. The whole area of Whitchurch throbbed with spiritual concern, living theology, chapel and strict Sabbath keeping. Taking into account the bleakness and remoteness of these communities set among the rural hills and mountains, cut off from the attractions of the every day world, it is a place for the soul to develop with God. There is a stillness about the whole place, away from the distractions of the fast moving world. Rev D Tyssul Evans, who also came from Foel Drigarn, wrote about the people of Whitchurch, describing those who inhabited these remote parts where there was no railway, no telegraph, no postal service – *there are few parts of the principality that are more distinctly Welsh in speech, dress, customs and manners.*[46] However, it was this environment which was to play a key part in shaping the character of many preachers. This area was fertile ground a hundred and fifty years ago for the growing of Gospel ministers.

Tyssul Evans, who wrote the only biography of Caleb Morris, describes him in these terms. *He was original in the sense of genuine individualism and he was true to himself. He had an intellect that saw in the Scriptures something that others could not see, and an emotional nature that felt in some respects what no other heart could feel and he spoke those thoughts and feelings in cadences, all his own cadences, which in his case were remarkably musical and thrilling. He had a royal nature and his endowments, both physical and mental, were all of the highest order.* One aspect of Caleb's ministry was the ability to feel. He felt from experience what he preached. He was able to enter into the pit of despair and the ecstasy of glory. When he preached, it was not only that he explained and unfolded the text, he felt it, and was able to bring before the congregation through his emotion, temperate seriousness, gracefulness, joy, fear, hope and glory as to the ways of God. Long before Philips Brooks penned the term *preaching is truth through personality*, Caleb Morris was a man who embodied that concept. It was also said he took the art of preaching to a new dimension.

Coming to Narberth as a student from Carmarthen College, he found the ideal place for a Welshman to develop. Tabernacle was a branch of the Welsh Independent Church at Henllan. The meetings at Tabernacle were held in Welsh as well as in English, but as the town became more English it was the place where Caleb learned to preach in a foreign tongue. He was a gifted preacher who had an impact on the locality but sadly he was only there three years before he was called to London. He learned to 'fly' in the Tabernacle pulpit and he soon 'flew off' to the largest and leading Congregational Church, at Fetter Lane, London. The history of Fetter Lane can be traced back to its founding Ministers, namely, leading puritans Dr Thomas Goodwin and Richard Baxter. When Caleb Morris arrived to take his position as Minister of Fetter Lane, it was said he shook London with his preaching and created a new era in the history of preaching. There was *a stately seriousness in his ministry. He felt that frivolity dishonoured the pulpit.* What would he think of today's preachers?

We have a feel of his preaching with the closing words of one of his sermons: *In conclusion let me but add that both the age and ourselves must soon appear before the God of all ages. What have we done in our age? Have we done anything? What do we purpose to do? Let us at once search ourselves. Let us work while it's day, for the shadows of night are fast gathering around us.* [47] Having served faithfully his age and generation with his great powers, he fell asleep and now lies peacefully at the foot of Foel Drigarn mountain. Benjamin Thomas, bardic name Myfyr Emlyn, said of him: *he was one of the greatest men I ever knew: a man in whose company one would derive in half an hour more benefit than in half an eternity at the feet of many who occupy theological chairs in our colleges. There was more theology in the squint of his eye than there is today in all the dry longwinded and formal lectures of many an old dry-as-dust Domini.*

This was no empty statement made by Benjamin Thomas for he knew him better than most, and Benjamin Thomas, in his own generation knew what it was to stand second to none. In the hall of famous Welsh preachers, Benjamin Thomas stood head and shoulders above his fellows in originality of thought and rhetorical ability. He met with Caleb on a number of occasions and was brought up in his shadow. Caleb was a hero to him and Benjamin would have heard the locals speak of Caleb as he grew up on the same mountainside by

Penygroes. Born at Ty-Rhos, Whitchurch, in a small cottage with a thatched roof, he was the seventh of eight children given to David and Elizabeth Thomas. His brother, Stephen Thomas, also became a well-known Baptist minister. Benjamin's father was one of the founders of Bethabara in 1826, originating from a Sunday School that was held in their house at Ty-Rhos. His father was converted in one of the local revivals and had an experience of salvation and became a great man of prayer and a faithful deacon to his grave. Benjamin's parents were not wealthy and life on those hills was hard. But wealth is not what you have in possessions. The family was both rich with God as well as in the home and community life.

Benjamin Thomas, like Caleb Morris, often made his way back to the foothills of Foel Drigarn to recharge his spiritual batteries and replenish his own well. There was a quality about these two men. They both knew God and the ways of God. Having been brought up in those parts, they were experts on the two books God has given - His Holy Word and the Book of Nature. They saw no contradiction between the two. The God who wrote was the God who created. When reading the writings, sermons, hymns and poems of Benjamin Thomas, it is evident he knew how to look at nature. He could look at a flower or a bird and learn more of God's ways. His instructor was the Master, the Lord Jesus, who spoke about seeds, trees, water, stones and mountains and made them come alive with heavenly thought. It was to these hills of Preseli that Benjamin would come back time and time again. It gave tone and colour to his life. He writes:

Joyous and frolicking and young on the hill
And mad with delight, I remember it still
I played with the sunbeams and breezes and glee
I laughed at the Sun and the Sun laughed at me
I revelled in thunders and lightnings and storms
I never thought, dreamt of dangers nor thought of reforms.
Duty was little with sheep on the hill
And often that little I failed to fulfil.

Benjamin was blessed with a strong physique but he became seriously ill at the age of fifteen. He had moved away and followed in the steps of his brother to find work in the industrial town of Tredegar. It was at around this time that he was converted. Many times God draws us to himself in our weakness. He was different from this time on and was baptised by John Rowe at Shiloh, Tredegar. Benjamin returned home and soon afterwards was encouraged to preach. He was sent for training at a school kept by Dr George Rees at Fishguard, and was admitted in 1855 to the Baptist College of Haverfordwest and then in 1858 to Bristol College. He was ordained at Dre-fach and Graig and remained there for thirteen years. He later moved on to Penarth, Cardiff, in 1873, but sighed for his native home. He grasped the chance to come to Narberth, his final move, in 1875, where the last scene of his life was played out.

At Narberth he was at the height of his powers, a patriarchal figure residing at Rushacre, the home of the founding Baptist, Griffith Howell, and from there the Bard sang like a nightingale. His wings were free and God had endowed him both naturally and spiritually. He was a child of nature and a child of God, a Minister of the Gospel, a preacher, lecturer, hymn-writer, orator, and poet - by the bardic name of Myfyr Emlyn. He was a popular Eisteddfod conductor, a passion of his life, and an author of some of the most popular books in the Welsh language, [48] a Bible commentator and the only Welsh preacher to contribute to the Pulpit Bible Commentary. It was said that *if he were English and a Methodist we would not have heard the last of it.* Editor of Seren Cymru (Welsh Baptist periodical), he was a patriot; Wales was in his heart and his heart was in Wales. He was a man of many parts and a prominent preacher. He was called upon to lecture and did so on a tour in America in 1880, on *Memories of the famous Welsh Pulpit, including such as Dafydd Evans of Ffynonhenry & Owen Griffiths of Gelli and founder of Blaenconin.*[49] These books became very popular and were reprinted in many editions. They are very amusing and full of humour. One of Myfyr's great gifts was that he could make the people laugh and cry in the same moment.

In 1868-9 he helped found the Church at Cwmduad. He was married twice,[50] his first wife was Margaret George of Baily Farm, Newcastle Emlyn, a member of the Graig Church, *a girl from the banks of the Teifi*, as he referred to her. They had five children and she died suddenly at the age of forty-two whilst visiting the family at Baily Farm. She never returned to Narberth and was buried at Cilfawr graveyard. Benjamin died on November 20th 1893. He was fifty-seven years of age and was buried at Bethesda. He had the largest funeral Narberth had ever seen. An epitaph is found in Bethesda with the words, *he faithfully and zealously served the Master.* On his tombstone you read *it is not the falling to the ground but the ascending of a Star.*

But it was as a preacher that he stood out. There were half a dozen occasions in his life when no one could compare with him - although he was compared to the one-eyed preacher, Christmas Evans. In 1863, at the age of 27, he preached at Blaenffos *The Wedding Feast of the Lamb.* For the locals, in such moments as these, God came upon the preaching and these occasions became marked historical events. It was not long before crowds came to hear "Ben Bach", as they called him.

One of his most famous sermons *Chariots of Salvation* he preached at the beginning of his ministry and on the big occasions such as Association Meetings. A description is given of "Ben Bach" preaching as a younger Minister in special services. First is the *strangeness* of the text that gripped the attention *Thou did ride upon Thine horses and Thy chariots of salvation.* Then there was the presence of the preacher and the fact that he was known to them as a homegrown boy. He began by describing the way saints of the Bible saw God - as sitting, as walking, but here "riding". He began to expound how *the Almighty is ever active in His universe. Although He is the one who is immovable and unchanging, He is ever the same, yesterday, today and forever; He is ever moving onward. In the theology of men, God is inactive, unconcerned, a passive observer, a mere onlooker. They say He has made this world. He has wound it up like a clock and left it for the laws of nature to govern, but Creation is full of His activity from the smallest atom to the sweeping planets.* [51] People at this point were looking intently in wonder as he described the atheistic view of nature as laws and forces - like horses without a rider. What a terrible sight, a dismal and distressing idea, and we know the pain of it today. However, the Christian sees God as riding His creation. He governs the thinking of His creatures by His Son and Spirit and Holy Word. He governs the heart of humanity. Benjamin goes on to say that *God comes with a message of salvation, as this text teaches. Chariots come for destruction and bloodshed. These are chariots of Salvation.* As he reaches the climax, *when the Prince of life, the Lord Jesus Christ, speaks to the charioteer: proceed to that speck you see on the confines of creation, which is the world. He came to this world bearing news of a Redeemer. He came doing good and bearing the cross and taking the handwriting that was against us and entering His chariot to the sky. But it is not the last. He is coming again, riding on the clouds the self-same chariots. If you trust in Him he will take you up to God.* By this time the chapel is filled with an "Amen" from the whole congregation.

David Davies describes one Sunday evening, the last time he heard Benjamin Thomas at Bethesda, Narberth. A thunderstorm had suddenly visited the district. The preacher was so moved by this phenomenon that within half an hour of the service he changed the text and preached from the words *God thunders marvellously with his voice.* The preacher, Benjamin, began to speak on the different voices of God. Among others was the voice of thunder. The heavens were meanwhile ablaze with lightning and rent with the crash of the elements. Catching the spirit of the storm, the preacher spoke in words of surpassing eloquence and overwhelming force of God's voice in the storms of life. At length, as if the elements without competed with the preacher in the pulpit, who was giving due adequate evidence to the truth, there came a quick succession of deafening claps of thunder and blinding flashes of lightning with such great force and intensity until at last, in one terrific outburst of power, the building was shaken to its very foundations. Thomas stood erect in the pulpit, like some ancient prophet or lawgiver, amid the thunderings and lightnings of Sinai, then spoke the intensely solemn and prophetic words *Hark, when the Master speaks it behoves His servant to be silent.* He sat down.

We have an idea of his sermon outlines from the Pulpit Commentary series. He was asked to send some samples for this commentary to Sir Robertson Nicoll. Within a few days the reply came back *gems of real worth, send as many as you like.* His sermon outlines numbered some 170,000 words. In these outlines, glimpses and insights of the Saviour are brought out through the Word of God, which are not found in the writings of other commentators. It was this focus on the person of Christ that makes his contribution so outstanding. An example is taken from John 15.11: *that my joy may remain in you.* He goes on to describe the joy the Lord Jesus had.

(a) **The joy of *conscious union with his Father.*** He was ever conscious of this. It never left him, even in the darkest hour and severest trials: *Ye shall leave me alone: but I am not alone, because the Father is with me.* This ever filled him with confidence and joy.

(b) **The joy of *perfect obedience.*** Obedience to his Father's will and commands, loyalty to his Father's throne, and consecration of his Father's work. It was the obedience of love. He could say, *Lo, I come to do.* It was delightful to come and do the Divine will while the law was in His heart of love.

(c) **The joy of *perfect love.*** Love to His Father, to His disciples, and love of compassion to the world. The central passion of His heart and the ruling law of his nature was love, and this inevitably produced happiness. There is no joy without love and He is love.

(d) **The joy of *perfect self-sacrifice.*** The love of Christ is not of the ordinary kind, but of the highest kind — the greatest, resulting in the greatest self-sacrifice. And the greater the self-sacrifice the greater the joy. In Christ it is more blessed to give than to receive.

(e) **The joy of *unswerving confidence of triumph and success.*** He never had the least doubt as to the ultimate success of His mission and the result of His coming, although no one was ever so severely tried. His own people rejected and crucified Him; but, in spite of this, His joy was unruffled, His happiness was unmarred, and His confidence in God the Father and the justice and success of His cause was unshaken — the joy of union with the Father, of obedience to Him and His commands, of love to Him and each other, of self-sacrifice even to suffering and death for Him, and of perfect conviction of the righteousness and complete triumph at last.

With natural and spiritual gifts, Benjamin Thomas had insight into the central core of the Christian faith and had a knowledge of and devotion to Christ. Lesser men fail to understand genius and were suspicious of him, perhaps because it was not in his nature to be narrow-minded, and we assess him by our own small standards. Benjamin did not see the dangers of the new modern critical scholarship and supported the centralisation of the training Colleges to the secular Universities of Wales. He was man of his time and his sermons capture the Romantic period. He had the powers of poetry, reason, history, philosophy and politics. During the elections he would compose songs that were heard on every street corner, shaking the dominion of the Tories. *His political speeches broke the chains of violence and oppression.* [52] No man was more active in the religious, political and cultural life of this land.

He was a man who lit his own fire on his own hearth. To use another phrase, from the Book of Proverbs, *he drew from his own well.* To draw from your own well shows a depth of life. His interests, his words, sermons and poems were not drawn from another source or another's experience but from his own walk and his knowledge of God. There was freshness in his being, something of the child and the angel. The message he preached was no echo of another age. He was a voice! Benjamin was alive in every way. He entered in-depth into joys and sorrows. Many fail in life not as Christians but rather as human beings. This will not be said of him. His life was tasted with all its sour sweetness. After Benjamin Thomas had been moulded, the mould was broken. He admired Caleb but never imitated him. Benjamin Thomas was gentle and quiet, although also as brave as a lion, yet as gentle as a lamb and innocent as a dove. In the obituary by his friends they said *he was a great personality in every sense. He was a genius. Possibly the only genius we have had in Wales!* [53] At least, that was the opinion of his friends.

Caleb Morris

Joseph is a fruitful bough, a fruitful bough near a spring whose Branches climb over a wall

Genesis 49 : 22

Its Branches Reach To The Sea

The late 18th and 19th centuries saw the consolidation of local chapels in Narberth. The eyes of their leaders and members turned from the woods, green hedgerows and fields that surrounded them, to other towns and cities, to dusty plains and parched lands that had never heard the Gospel: to mission.

Both Caleb Morris and Benjamin Thomas had ministries reaching far beyond Narberth. The field of pastoral care lay beyond the confines of Tabernacle's chapel doors. In the three years of Caleb's ministry at Narberth, regular meetings were conducted in the surrounding villages, with cottage and field meetings. For Caleb, a typical Sunday would consist of preaching in the morning at Tabernacle, a field meeting at Llandissilio in the afternoon and a preaching service in the evening. Old local chapels, such as Carven and Sardis, Kilgetty, knew of help and assistance in the pastoral oversight given by Caleb. Between 1835 and 1849 Benjamin Thomas of Whitley served as moderator of Molleston on a number of occasions and his successor, William Richard Owen, held almost a bishop-type ministry, looking after the local Baptist causes in the district.

In 1818, three of the most well known Baptist Ministers were preaching at the Association Meetings at Molleston: they were Christmas Evans, John Herring and Dr John Ryland. [54] Their messages and concerns were for the need of prayer meetings and Sunday Schools. John Herring and Dr John Ryland were to be influential in the new missionary movement. William Carey, a Baptist cobbler from Northampton, was to become the father of modern mission resulting from a famous address *expect great things from God, attempt great things for God.* From its conception Missionary concern played a major part in the philosophy of Bethesda.

The stimulus for this concern can be traced through the themes of the annual meetings of the Association held at Bethesda in 1842, 1869,

Benjamin Thomas of Toronto
(Son of Benjamin Thomas, Whitley Farm)

1924, 1942 and 1964. *The Claims of Home and Foreign Mission Upon Us* by Rev E Williams, Aberystwyth in 1842; *Church Discipline* by the Rev John Harris, Pembroke, in 1869; *The Loyalty of the Church to Christ, Essential in her Efforts to Win the World* by Mr D Richards, Gilfach, Glanrhyd; *The Need for More Practical Religion in our Churches* by Mr Vincent Davies, Haverfordwest, in 1924; and *The Book that Refuses to Grow Old* by Rev T M Jones, Roch, in 1942.

The missionary atmosphere is stressed in a wonderfully coincidental manner by the fact that Bethesda was the venue of the Association conference when the Baptist Missionary Society celebrated its first Jubilee in 1842 and then its Tri-jubilee in 1942. Benjamin Evans was baptised here in 1865 and laboured for years in India. Many people from this town have gone throughout the world, spreading the message of light and forgiveness. What religious fervour there must have been in this small town! Large congregations, seminary schools, missionaries and big preachers, with early morning prayer meetings!

Narberth Chapels were to be a blessing both nationally and internationally during the ministry of Henry Davies. He was the longest serving Minister of Tabernacle, who taught and prepared a number of students for ministry and mission, averaging 8 - 12 at a time. Among those taught was the Rev Evan Thomas of Tiers Cross and Rosemarket. A number went to the mission field, for example, George Palmer Davies BA of the Foreign Bible Society, went firstly to Berlin and then to Switzerland. He later died in Berlin. There is a tablet in Tabernacle dedicated to him. He displayed great ability and rendered important service to the German Army in the Franco–German War, distributing some hundreds of thousands of Bibles among the soldiers. The Emperor Frederick invited him to his Castle, where he received the special thanks of the Emperor on behalf of the Society. His service was cut short by overwork but his wife remained in Berlin and carried on Christian witness among the cabmen of the city.

Rev James Thomas was another local lay preacher who went onto the missionary field. A native of Saundersfoot, he was received into membership and began his preaching ministry at Tabernacle before being ordained as a missionary to serve in Shanghai, China. He went out and returned a few years later, in 1878, to become one of the District Secretaries of the British and Foreign Bible Society. Rev John Hughes was also a pupil of Henry Davies. He left Narberth at the age of 17 and made a name for himself as a preacher by becoming Pastor of one of the leading and most influential pulpits in the country. Others include Rev H Mathias, Wolfedale; the Rev Fred Fox Thomas, St Florence and Harrogate; the Rev D Salmon, Pembroke; the Rev Thomas Davies, Cardigan; the Rev David Davies, Llanelli; the Rev G B Morris and the Rev Dan E Evans. To think of the influence and importance of raising such a number of men to the ministry, from one small town, giving their lives over to the service of the kingdom of God now seems amazing.

Tabernacle had a number of Ministers who went from Narberth to be a force for good in the cities of this country and overseas. One such minister was Joseph Morris, who left Narberth for larger fields of pasture and settled in Brunswick Chapel, Bristol. Then after a number of years he became pastor of an important church at Ilfracombe, where his ministry prospered over many years. His brother, the Rev William Edward Morris, went out from Tabernacle as a missionary to Tirupoor, India. Both he and Maurice Phillips, of Aberdare, were ordained at Tabernacle on August 4th 1861; Maurice eventually became known as "Phillips of Madras". Morris, before he went to India, was used of God in this town by conducting a very flourishing Bible class and it attracted many members from other denominations also. W M Howell, a young boy of 15, came under deep conviction and was converted under the ministry of Joseph Morris. He then joined the Church and preached his first sermon in 1858, before going and serving at Frampton Cotterel near Bristol.

John Morlais Jones was another Minister who came to Tabernacle and went on to greater things. He came from Llangennech, near Llanelli, and was ordained at Tabernacle in 1865. However, like his predecessor, Caleb Morris, he stayed for only three years then moved to the London metropolis to become Minister of Lewisham Congregational Church. He preached for nearly a quarter of a century before publishing a sermon. His sermons were full of profound evangelical truth. Eventually, he became a leader in the denomination. There was a tablet placed in Tabernacle in his Memory:

JOHN MORLAIS JONES

Who for three years was Minister of this Church, and 32 years Minister of the Congregational Church Lewisham, London. He persuaded many by his rare eloquence to the imitation of Jesus Christ. He was Chairman of the London Congregational Union of England and Wales for 1897 and he died 26th September 1905, aged 62.

W Alonzo Griffiths was yet another preacher from Tabernacle, a fiery, stern preacher whose desire was to see men saved. His theology was soundly evangelical. One could describe him as having something of John the Baptist in his fearless reproof of sin. If sometimes he erred by over severity, it proceeded from an earnest desire to save men. He later became a Minister of the Congregational Church in Sketty, Swansea. An extract of his preaching is found from his sermons preached in London – *Nine tenths of the world's unbelief springs from the heart, not from the head. The plea of honest doubt in the majority of cases is very dishonest, and the plain truth is they love darkness rather than light. Sin may be clasped so close we cannot see its face. Samson perished under the ruins of his prison – why? Was it for want of evidence? I know not. His bursting lust for Delilah brought him to that vulgar, shameful end. Demas turned his back upon the Redeemer and forsook Paul and the Churches when they greatly needed his sympathy and help. Was it doubts that caused his apostasy? No - 'he loved the present world' your iniquities have separated between you and God.* [55] He loved the Church, and therefore could not bear in it those who were evil.

John Albert Thomas had the unenviable task of following Benjamin Thomas at Bethesda. His stay was for six years, from 1894 to 1900. He moved often in his ministry but it can be said that his Churches, Nantgwyn, St Mellons, Bethlehem, Salem, and Narberth held to a Gospel ministry throughout. Each of those Churches had a unique testimony of remaining true to the cause throughout a period of decline. Other notable men - David Griffiths, who became Principal of Accrington Baptist College, was a man who was faithful to the teachings of Grace. John Collins went to Bradford College and is buried in the grounds of Bethesda Chapel. There was as also Frederick C Tucker of Honeyboro, buried in Neyland 1908.

Many of the Ministers who have served here, perhaps for a few years, have also been a means of service to other places throughout the country. Following the ministries of these men and their places of appointment is an encouragement for us today, when many of our present chapels are on the brink of closure and have fallen into apostasy. However, many of these pastorates have also remained true to the gospel. I am not saying it is because, or in spite, of them but their works have followed them.

The mountains were covered with its shade the
mighty cedars with its branches.
It sent out its boughs to the sea its shoots as far as the river.

Psalm 80 : 11

Bethesda Baptist Church

The Rev. R. Menai Williams 1938—1945

A Root out of the Stem

A new century was to dawn and also a new era for the Church. General William Booth, founder of the Salvation Army, warned that the chief dangers confronting the coming century would *be religion without the Holy Ghost, Christianity without Christ, forgiveness without repentance, salvation without regeneration, politics without God and heaven without hell.* How true he was. What was once a vibrant Christian Church throughout the country had now become, in one way, a religion of the past and not having a living reality in the present.

By the last two decades of the 19th century, the presence of liberal and modernistic theology had taken hold. The Theological Colleges were centralised and a cold chill arrived as rationalistic teaching began to spread to such places as Narberth. By 1885 a down-grade controversy had gripped the Baptist denomination, when Charles Spurgeon stood up to contend for the faith that was *once and for all given to the saints* that was now being denied by those who filled the Ministerial Colleges and pulpits throughout the land. During Spurgeon's time some Welshmen stood with him and following his death people such as R B Jones sought to defend the evangelical faith. The articles of faith once fought for were now simply forgotten. With a greater scientific knowledge and an optimistic view of the world, the motto was *upwards and onwards* and man's confidence was in man, not God and His Word.

The spiritual temperature in the Church in Wales was of serious concern for some and the only answer to its decline came through what is now known as the 1904 Revival. Evan Roberts, who became the spearhead of the 1904 revival in Wales, was the most well known Welshman since King Arthur! Locally, the Welsh speaking communities were more affected namely Blaenconin, with six converts; Maenclochog, with sixteen, and Whitland, with twenty-four. During the month of January a further sixty were added to the list from this area. Narberth did not miss the blessing. It was reported in the Western

Mail that the number of conversions here between 8th - 31st December was twenty-eight.

Some have questioned the lasting effects of this revival and asked why the spiritual decline in the chapels was not halted with this national outpouring of God's Grace. One of the contributing factors was the 1st World War. The cenotaph in Market Square pays tribute to those from Narberth and Crinow North who fell, with few returning without some scar. The war brought with it many questions. The optimism had gone but so had the once-united faith of the Nonconformist Congregations. With the depression of the 1920's - 1930's and then another World War, with all of its social and political upheaval, the challenges were immense. With the Biblical faith being undermined, power and authority had departed. The year 1928 was to register the first year of decline amongst the Baptist denomination membership and there has never been a year since with a higher total than the preceding year.

Having taken up the pastorate of Bethesda in 1903, and despite the blessings of 1904, Rev W E Stephens could never have anticipated the extent of change during his association with the Chapel, both as Minister until 1935 and as a member until his death in 1958. He is buried in the Bethesda Chapel graveyard and gave his life to its cause when answering the call to Bethesda whilst he was at Blaina Baptist. Although he was dear to them there they reluctantly let him go and showed their affection with a gift of an oak writing desk and drawers which was made-to-measure for the new Manse, then still at the old dwelling of Rushacre.

He is the third Minister of the Church to have a tablet erected in his memory. The impression his sermons made would live on with those who heard him. Dr Henton Davies, who took the radio service from Bethesda in 1945, said of Stephens *he was conservative and orthodox in his beliefs.*

W E Stephens was a fine preacher, having all the gifts of the orator but also being a good pastor. When he stepped down from office, the chapel presented him with a monetary gift for his faithful service. It is a testimony to the close bond and affection in which he was held by those he had pastored over the years that a grand sum of £131.15 was given - the equivalent of £5,000 in today's value - and it was given at the time of the great depression. There was a strong, loving relationship between the pastor and people.

Many churches made approaches to him to be their Minister but he refused them all. He had been asked many times the reason as to why he had remained in Narberth so long. His reply to that question was that during 1911, when he had sustained a long and serious illness, the Church at Bethesda had remained true to him, and in return he could only remember their kindness by remaining true to his Church, which he loved so much. The steadfast commitment of the members to their Minister has been a key to the chapel's continued existence to this day. He seldom went elsewhere to preach and never bothered with committees or Baptist Association meetings, it was to Bethesda he was called and to his own flock he tended.

One of the differences between Bethesda and Tabernacle has been the longevity of service by their Ministers. W E Stephens had a steady ministry that saw the Church through the great changes and difficulties of the early 20th century. It may not have been the spirited ministry of the great Myfyr Emlyn but it was faced with challenges and pressures of social, theological and economical concerns. During the Great War, sixty-four members of the Church served in the forces and eight of them made the supreme sacrifice.

But entertainment rather than preaching was becoming more prominent, with singing festivals and concerts starting to become the main diet of Church life throughout Wales. The idea of the chapel as being the place set apart for the Word of God to be preached and prayer to be made (as mentioned in the deeds) was lost. Other activities and social events were now very much part of Church life, the idea being that chapels were the few places that had room for public events and were now looked at not only as the centre for spiritual life but also the social life of the community. The Bible was no longer central. Talent nights and social, rather than spiritual, events prevailed for example,

Christmas day was spent gathered in the schoolroom with the children playing games.

It is interesting to note the *Declaration of our Fundamental Principles, prominent in a small handbook given to new Church members at this time: Believing, professing, and maintaining the important doctrines of the one living and true God; three equal persons in the Godhead; the proper Deity and real Humanity of our Lord Jesus Christ; Eternal and Personal Election; Original Sin; Particular Redemption; Free Justification by the imputed Righteousness of Christ; Regeneration, Conversion and Sanctification by the Spirit and the Grace of God; the Moral Law a rule for the conduct of all believers; the Final Perseverance of the Saints; the Resurrection of the Dead; the Future Judgement; the Eternal Happiness of the Righteous, and the Endless Misery of such as die Impenitent; and practising Baptism by Immersion in Water, in the name of the Father, and the Son and the Holy Ghost, to such only as are of years of understanding upon their confession of Repentance towards God and Faith in our Lord Jesus Christ.*

Picture houses became the latest novelty and this visual means of communication began taking over from the God-ordained verbal form of preaching. Such changes promoted discussion in the then midweek Guild Meetings of the Church. One senses the tension that Stephens felt between the sacred and secular with the installation of the new organ in 1906, costing £230. In the press report of this grand occasion, Stephens reminds the congregation that they had not come to a concert but to worship God. The day after, being a Sunday, with a packed chapel full of people having come to hear the organ for the first time, Stephens took as his theme the worship of God as the highest calling of humankind and that *if the heart is not right there is no instrument that can make one's worship right with God.* [56] The adding of an organ to the worship of chapel services was a contentious issue. When Tabernacle installed their first organ the then incumbent of St Andrew's considered this as competition, making the gibe that *next they will have a choir.*

Mary Rochester records in *My Father was a Narberth Man* how one of her relatives, John Thomas (Senior Deacon), would majestically announce the hymns, but read the whole hymn right through to the end before the organ could play. Mary adds the comment *no one suggested that this was carrying things too far,* [57] not realising that this was a custom and belief that the words needed to be thought about before they were sung. It was the word and not the musical feelings that were important.

Interestingly, with an advertisement in the Narberth and Whitland News, July 30th 1908, announcing the forthcoming Anniversary Service on 2nd August, an air of jubilant expectancy heralded the coming of the Rev D J Hiley, who was known throughout the land as the most eminent of Baptist Ministers. It says *that although he has held high places in the field, he is still in the zenith of his popularity and is as vigorous as ever in the proclamation of the evangel of the cross. Mr Hiley's ministry has always been generously evangelical and with Christ as its centre.*[58] This is an indication of the life and temperature of the spiritual climate of Bethesda - but these are only glimpses among the myrtle trees. The interesting feature of this article was the description of the preacher: *his ministry has always been generously evangelical. He is as vigorous as ever in his proclamation of the cross and with Christ as the centre.*

There were those in the congregation who truly had an experience and belief in the old Gospel. The doctrine of the remnant was true in Bethesda and it remained true for the next sixty years despite apostasy taking place. Newspaper accounts of the church life from 1920-1930 tell the story that, instead of Bible study, debate took precedence. The Bible had its place but was not so prominent any longer. One elderly lady remembered to her last days the distinctive divide there had been between Church and Chapel, with her testimony that the Baptists were much keener and more zealous in the practice of their faith and had to be admired. In her eyes, however, they were of a lower social class and she was taught to have nothing to do with them.

Bethesda Chapel at that time was still the largest Baptist cause numerically in the Pembrokeshire Association, with two hundred and fifteen members back in 1921, rising to a peak of two hundred and fifty eight members in 1958. A number of great preachers came from these parts and then returned to preach. One occasion to note was the return of the Rev Thomas Phillips, whose home chapel was Rhydwilym, and who became a prominent Minister of Bloomsbury Baptist Church between 1905-1928, the social work of which gathered wide attention. However, being from these parts, his boyhood experience was filled with stories of Welsh Revivals and he had taken an interest in the happenings of 1904. When he came to Bethesda, it was the highlight of Baptist church life and the sanctuary was filled to capacity, with many sitting on the steps leading to the gallery.

It is never easy to follow a long ministry but a man who made a mark within a few years was Menai Richard Williams. He was a fine preacher and pastor with a great devotion to Christ. The proclamation of the Gospel was the passion of his life. He had a winsome personality and even today the congregation here remembers stories of him at Bethesda. Some found his manner and preaching challenging but the commitment he showed to Christ was an example to all. His ministry was to cover the hardest years of the 20th century, 1938-45 when men from this town were away fighting and serving. At every prayer meeting each and every person serving in the armed forces was named and prayed for. Williams had a love and compassion for people and made the headlines of the newspaper when he gave the shoes he was wearing to a tramp by the side of the road near Sodston Farm. There was truly a glimpse of the Saviour during his time in the pulpit. He would often break out with the hymn... *Were you there when they crucified my Lord ? Were you there when they nailed him to the tree? Were you there when he rose up from the dead?* He was a recognised preacher and was asked to submit one of his sermons in a book called *Young Preachers in Wales.* There were some, it is sad to say, who did not know the day of visitation and thought Menai to be too zealous in his out-working of the life of Christ. The eulogy concerning him could not have been higher: *A servant had come among them and he was taken.* As some would say, he was too zealous in his love of the

Saviour and this was an unsettling experience for the congregation. *He had a passion to serve the Master; preaching was his forte. He had the eye, heart and mind of the true servant of the Word.* [59]

During the War, children came from London and other major cities to be evacuated here in Narberth and consequently the chapel schoolroom was used as a school for them. Many have left their names carved into the pews of the chapel. These were indeed times of strain both emotionally and spiritually, with men away at war and children away from their parents. Tea parties were organised at Bethesda for those who later returned from the war and eventually a big homecoming for Mr Tommy Adams, member of Bethesda, returning home after spending six years in a prisoner of war camp in Poland.

As previously mentioned, Dr Henton Davies gave a BBC radio broadcast from Bethesda in 1946. It was recorded in the morning and transmitted that same evening. People stayed away from church specifically to listen to it. Henton was one of the leading Baptist men at that time and was Principal of Regent's Park Baptist College, Oxford. In his sermon for the occasion, he illustrated how a beachhead had been made for the Allies to land and take a foothold on the shores of Normandy. Likewise, he said *the mission of Christ sent from heaven to make a beachhead for God to come and set up His Kingdom on earth.* Such illustrations were fresh in the minds of the congregation and would have especially struck a chord with them. This sermon is a good example of what preaching was going to be like for the next forty years in the pulpits of our land. Scholarly, Biblical, orthodox but not necessarily believed by those who preached. It lacked the vital message that we have redemption through Christ's blood and the forgiveness of sins. It was as William Booth had prophesied fifty years before – *a religion without atonement, without regeneration, without repentance and faith, without the need for new birth.*

War once again had left not only a physical scar but also spiritual and social scars. During the war people made their way to the prayer meetings but after this, Frank Goodwin commented in 1948 on the decline of the prayer meeting. He argued publicly for commitment by writing about this need in the newspaper. God was to be gracious to Bethesda. Frank was a young man who had recently converted from Roman Catholicism; he later went on to a successful ministry in London and became president of the Baptist Union of Great Britain. Being a young convert to Christ, Frank had an evangelistic message and ministry, he won people to the Lord and to the Church. One tale, which has been told and retold, with many variations over time is that one particular Sunday night, after having preached, Frank felt compelled to make an appeal for people to come to Christ. His last version of the account was the most dramatic but perhaps not the most accurate as Frank said his memory was fading. Nevertheless, this is what he retold at the funeral of Mrs Betty Martin, who at one time led the Sunday School here at Bethesda. After having the compulsion to make the appeal and feeling sure it was from the Lord, it was to his dismay that no one responded. However, he remained in the pulpit until everyone had gone. As he sat there with only the light of the pulpit visible he heard footsteps coming up the path and then the door opening. It was Betty. She had been moved to confess Christ earlier but had not responded. Sadly, his ministry was only for three years, although people were added to the church during his period of office. In 1952 there were two hundred and sixty members still on the books. Throughout the fifties Bethesda was one of, if not, the largest Church in the Association. By 1958, when Bethesda celebrated its 150th Anniversary, it had two hundred and fifty eight members. This was a grand occasion that lasted an entire week during the month of September. Rev D Bowen had been the Minister for the previous six years, from 1949–55, while the Rev Wynn Evans had taken up the pastorate the year before, in 1957.

The 1960's were just around the corner and a social revolution was to take place, questioning the order and norms that a previous generation had taken for granted. The authority of the Bible had been undermined for the previous fifty years and the church was unarmed and unprepared for the tough questions posed by the new rock-and-roll generation. Science was looked to for the answers: The rise of the hippy culture saw the embracing of eastern religion, challenges to institutions, and espousal of liberal ideas. Only the strongest churches committed to the Word of God survived and stood during those years. Adding to the spiritual decline, Narberth was to see the effect of economic and social changes.

Frank Goodwin & Deaconate in 1948

Back Row
John Adams, Leslie Roberts, Tom Adams, James Thomas and George Edwards

Front Row
Daniel Hitchings, John Lewis, Rev Frank Goodwin, Cyril Owen and William Williams

Far from being the busy, thriving, shopping community that it is today and once was, now with the closure of the mart as well as the grammar school, the recession of the 80's saw young people move away for work. Narberth was not the place for a thriving, flourishing ministry. The elderly congregations reflected much of the past but also of the present situation, that of an aging community.

Rev W J Howells ministered during these most difficult of days. He came from Cardiff in 1963, retiring in 1990. The rich Christian history of the past was only a memory at the turn of the 21st century and, to a new generation and newcomers to the town, it was now lost and forgotten. It is recorded in the Bible: *there rose a king over Egypt that did not know Joseph and all he did for good for that people.* [60] The town by this time had become affluent and with it the truth of the saying *where poverty had killed its thousands, prosperity spiritually speaking its tens of thousands,* was seen to be true.

Over the last twenty years, laws concerning Sunday trading have been passed without regard to our Risen Lord. When the first shop in Saundersfoot opened its doors one Sunday in 1954 it was met with a protest from the local Chapels, Bethesda included, sending their letter of concern to those in authority. Today the streets of Narberth are busy on Sundays, not with worshippers but with shoppers and people in the local public houses watching the sport. Change in the Sunday laws in the last decade of the 20th century has hastened the decline of the religious culture of the land.

By the time of the bi-centenary, membership of Bethesda had fallen once more to fifty-eight and, during 2009, it became the last Nonconformist cause left in the town. Since the 1970's in Wales, every single week one Nonconformist cause has closed its doors for the last time. By 1960, there were approximately sixty-eight thousand Baptists in the Welsh Union but the number by 2008 was fourteen thousand and still falling. Not even the local Church in Wales has been spared and it has been nearly a 100 years since both Priest and Curate pastored the parish. Long gone are the days when 150 would gather for evensong. The effects of liberal and modernistic theology have had a devastating effect on the whole of religious life.

In speaking of the glimpses of Christ amongst His people, one can still testify that even in these dark and depressing days of 'dead religion', God has not been left without a witness. The presence of Christ is still in the witness and life of this town. Although things were dark, God had his people in this town and in Bethesda itself. There were those left who had been in the Church for years, which had come to faith, and were like flowers in a desert land kept only by God and who remained faithful and true. An example of this during these years was the work of the Baptist Missionary Society and the local Baptist Association who would organise Youth Camps. From these camps a number of young people came to faith. One who gave testimony to this was Norma Bates, who spoke one Sunday night at Bethesda Chapel, saying that some fifty years earlier she had been in one of these camp meetings and prayed that the Lord would save her. Her evidence that a change had taken place was, that whilst others left the Sunday School and Chapel in teenage years, Norma was baptized, having been encouraged to take the step by members after witnessing a change in her life.

Stories have been recounted of those who, from the pew, would challenge the errors of the preachers and who would ensure that preachers who did come to minister would be Gospel men with a message.

Throughout this time, God had His witnesses for the Anniversary Services and Sunday School. Men would be chosen who would tell about the Christ they loved. These meetings were longed for and looked forward to. Men such as I D E Thomas, the speaker for the Anniversary Services of 1958; Emrys Davies from Mount Pleasant, was a favourite and Russell Jones of Risca. Local Ministers such as Hywel Jones of Letterston and Cecil Jenkins of Llwynhendy all came. There were but a few who were well known evangelicals who made their way to the pulpit at Bethesda but there were still people who wanted to hear of their Saviour.

In 1964, the last of the great Association meetings were held at Bethesda, over three days and beginning with prayer meetings at nine o' clock in the morning. The theme was, *The Unchanging Christ*. Dr Martyn Lloyd-Jones, the famous Welsh preacher from London, preached at least once (if not more) at Tabernacle.

One person to note who made a great stir for the gospel and lived in Narberth during the seventies was Dr Peter Trumper, who started a work in Clarbeston Road and served as a Protestant Truth Preacher for Wales; Dr Martyn Lloyd-Jones said *"there is a young man in Pembrokeshire called Trump... Trump... Trump... Trumpet - and by all accounts, he's busy blowing it! Trumpeting forth the Gospel."* [61]

Lo amid the Myrtles standing one who merits all my love,
though but dimly I discern Him to excel all else above;
blessed morning when the shadows flee away.

Ann Griffiths 1776-1805

Tabernacle Chapel

Bethesda 150 years Anniversary 1958

1958—Bethesda Sunday School.

Conclusion

When I arrived here at Bethesda Chapel in 1995, my first recollection was of decay, both spiritually and physically. As an outsider, I remember the darkness of the then six lights hanging from the ceiling, held by the old brown cord wiring. The left-hand-side of the chapel building was badly in need of repair and there was no kitchen or carpet in the schoolroom. It was remarkable how the ladies fed three hundred people on two occasions on the day of my ordination. There were the faithful few who came Sunday by Sunday and who had kept the doors open when for five years previously there had been no Minister. The habit and instruction of former days and godly parents no doubt had planted a seed that would not die.

In 1995 I attended my first civic event in Narberth and the speaker for the occasion was Canon Hamer, then in his eighties, retired from the ministry of Maenclochog. I heard him preach for the one and only time. He emphasised the need for a new heart: *you need a new heart to be given to you which only Jesus can give*, and if no else heard then I did, for God lets none of his words fall to the ground. When I asked *how do you prepare?* He replied, *I make sure everything I say is the truth.* Narberth has always had glimpses of the Saviour and even if the Gospel has not always burned brightly it has burned enough for people to see the light and acknowledge that He is there. Other places of worship have since started up in the town. Some have continued and others have not, some have split and others have regrouped over the last 20 years.

During the first few years after my coming, the faithful from Church and Chapel would make their way on a Sunday night for evening worship. In Bethesda, there were elderly people who had a stamp upon them of the old ways of God, but time reaped its harvest during the 90's and all those who came for that evening service were soon taken to glory. For example, Mrs Jones, widow of a former Minister of Molleston, made it her place to support the work even though in her 90's. She had been converted at the age of eight, after her father had been converted during the 1904 revival. Tommy Adams, whose supportive word of encouragement was so needed, and Mrs Badham, were both such people who knew the sound of the old message in their younger day and were glad to hear the old tune again this side of heaven. Violet Griffiths served as Deacon, Sunday School teacher and Sisterhood President; prayed faithfully and was taken home in 1996. It was the faithful servants who kept the light flickering.

Back in the days when the Sunday School at Bethesda was strong and those who ran it knew the Lord, for example, Mr Tom Lewis, schoolteacher, Joan Morgan, Mr A G Pitt, whose witness remained with the children – for some throughout their lives. One story comes to mind, which I heard during a pastoral visit to one of the men of the Church who had gone through those years of Sunday School. Although he had not followed himself, he told me the story of how Anthony Pitt said, *you could have everything in life but unless you knew Christ you will never be happy.* In my pastoral visit he said, *I never forgot those words and there is a truth in them.* Many from the Sunday School, although not in Narberth (having moved away to college and work) have come to a living faith in Christ and this is a witness to the Sunday School ministry.

The Sisterhood played a great part in keeping the doors of Bethesda open; meeting on a Wednesday afternoon and at one point more attended it than the Sunday services. Then there are those who are still with us and not mentioned for the very reason that it will be for another to continue and write our page in this glorious history. It is not our time of honour and glory. It is enough that we can say we have seen Him and, on many occasions, have experienced powerful visitations of Him in our meeting together at Bethesda.

The prayer meetings have once again been established as one of the main means of grace. Many who attended have testified what a blessing it has been to find a prayer meeting where people pray. As some have said, the prayer meeting is the powerhouse of the Church; this has been so true in the on-going life of the cause at Bethesda.

If the chapel history were continued to be written, it would be said of these closing years of the 20th century and the beginning of this 21st century, that the people called once again for God to revive His cause in the midst of the years.

Another significant spiritual development has been the focus on mission locally, nationally and internationally. The command to go into all the world and preach the Gospel has once again found a place in the hearts of those who worship at Bethesda. It all first came about from a connection with the Southern Baptist Churches in North Carolina. Over the years we have had links with Dunn, Asheboro and Winston Salem, who have sent teams to help us with evangelism. Their willingness to come has been a spur for us as a congregation to carry out this work locally, nationally and to send teams to Armenia. These two factors of prayer and evangelism have been the main means of God working in the midst of the Church.

Improvements have been made in the last 15 years to the structure and fabric of our building but also in the hearts of people. The seed has been watered, shoots of new life have appeared and that which was dry and lifeless has flowered and bloomed into life with new birth having been experienced; fruit has been borne of love, faith, repentance, and obedience to God. The word of command, *compel them to come in,* which is written above the organ has been a promise once again for the church in its mission and evangelistic work. There have been glimpses of the Saviour but we long for his abiding presence with us as in the days of old. Although the forest of Narberth has long been covered with concrete and houses now stand where there were once fields and trees, the seed planted by a generation of faithful witness will again bear fruit in abundance:

Instead of the thorn shall come up the cypress tree,
And instead of the brier shall come up the myrtle tree; and it shall be to the Lord for
a name, for an everlasting sign that shall not be cut off.

Isaiah 55 : 13

The Ladies Fellowship in 1996
An outing to Woodstock

200 year Anniversary in 2008

COME DOWN TO THIS BETHESDA

Come down to this Bethesda,
    May we Thy presence feel;
Come down to move the waters,
    Come down to help and heal;
Make it a "House of Mercy"
    And prayer, Lord, we crave;
Come down in all Thy glory,
    Almighty One, to save!

Come down to teach all ages
    Obedience to Thy rule;
Come down, Thou friend of children,
    And bless our Sunday School;
When we who built this temple
    Are come to Thee, by grace,
Oh! Help our children's children
    To worship in this place.

Our sainted friends in heaven
    Are near, though far away,
And in their snow-white garments
    Rejoice with us to-day;
With praise and adoration
    This happy day we see,
And dedicate this building
    With singing, Lord, to Thee.

Lord, we have built this temple,
    In honour of Thy name;
O fill it with Thy glory,
    And with the Saviour's fame.
May those who worship here
    All to Thy glory live;
And when we pray, Our Father,
    O answer and forgive.

Barddoniaeth Myfyr Emlyn
Written specifically and sung at the opening services of Bethesda Baptist Chapel, Narberth.
British Library 1608 6115

NOTES

1   Narberth Weekly News 7/6/28 describes pilgrims making their way to Rhydwilym, the birthplace of the Baptist cause. Surrounded by forest, those travelling to its spot were hidden from view until only yards from the assembly.

2   Luke 3 : 14; Luke 7 : 1-10; Philippians 1 : 13

3   Nero selected a group of the finest athletes and called them The Emperor's Wrestlers. These soldiers were often sent on special missions. On a certain campaign in Gaul (Modern France) many of them were converted and under the persecution of Nero 40 of them were sentenced to freeze to death on an iced-over lake.

4   Thomas Charles, CHRISTIANITY IN ROMAN BRITAIN TO AD 500 (B T BATSFORD LTD) published 1981 p43

5   Roman coins have been found near the town of Narberth and a Roman road was uncovered as far as Whitland during the by-pass road works in the 90's.

6   David Walker "A History of the Church in Wales. Church in Wales Publication 1977 p2.

7   The Norse men had come from Scandinavia and settled at what is now Dublin. There are unconfirmed reports that the Saxons & the Vikings sacked Narberth .

8   Narberth Weekly News 7.6.28.

9   The Journal of Pembrokeshire Historical Society Number 12.2003 p6.

10 The Story of Narberth p7. A description of this possible court that would have existed is given.

11 ibid p22.

12 Authorities on the history of the Perrot Family question the existence of this man.

13 Names of incumbents found inside St Andrews Narberth.

14 Gerald Of Wales The Journey Through Wales. The Description of Wales, Penguin 1978 p29.

15 The Story of Narberth p15.

16 Gwyn Davies "A light in the Land Christianity in Wales 200- 2000" Bryntirion Press 2002 p38.

17 It has long been thought that Wales had only three Martyrs, There was another whom little is known about, namely Oliver Richardie, who was burned at Haverfordwest 1555. (See: Roots of Reformed faith in Pemborkeshire, Haverfordwest Library).

18 A copy can be seen at Narberth Museum.

19 1650-60 Act for the Propagation of the Gospel in Wales.

20 Jenkins Geraint H. Protestant Dissenters in Wales 1639 – 1689. Cardiff University of Wales Press 1992 p44.

21 Richard Castle – Family appeared in Pembrokeshire during the Civil War and received grants of land in Narberth.

22 The 1689 list of names can be found at The National Library of Wales, Aberystwyth.

23 Story of Narberth p26.

24 The annual fair was held quarterly until 1792 and by 1850 it was held eight times a year, increasing to fifteen.

25 Griffith Stephen "A History of Quakers in Pembrokeshire" Gomer Press 2004 p13.

26 ibid p15.

27 Howel Harris in Pembrokeshire.

28   The Calvinistic Methodist Fathers of Wales, Volume One, John Morgan Jones and William Morgan, translated by John Aaron, The Banner of Truth Trust, 2008 p194.

29   ibid p194.

30   ibid p197.

31   ibid p202.

32   ibid p204.

33   ibid p296-207.

34   The Story of Narberth 2000 p33.

35   Historical article found by Dr Rees and can be read from the Church archives at Narberth Museum.

36   Experience meetings were at the spiritual centre of Methodist corporate life where people would come and share their spiritual journeys and real experiences of God.

37   Report unsure of location.

38   Deeds of Bethesda Chapel.

39   Rev T D Davies Bleanffos after four years followed by Rev D Griffths.

40   Thomas B D Sermons Toronto William Briggs 1911.

41   The Pubs of Narberth, Keith Johnson p105 Logaston Press 2004.

42   David Davies memoirs at Aberystwyth Library under Benjamin Thomas archives.

43   The Cup of Cold Water and other sermons by the Rev J Morlais Jones, London Low, Marston & company Limited St Dunstan's House Fetter Lane Fleet Street, 1894.

44   Jones Abel J, John Morgan MA Gomerian Press Llandyssul 1939.

45   Tombstone found in St Andrews Church to George Devonald Of Sodstone House who in his life time charged thirty pounds a year on the farm of Rushacre for the purpose of establishing a free school and schools in the parish to teach the poor children to read write and arithmetic. Died 1836.

46   Evans Tyssul biography of Caleb Morris, English edition 1902.

47   Caleb Morris Memorial by David Thomas DP Pulpit Memorials 1878 p411.

48   The biography of Dafydd Evans, Ffynonhenry. 15,000 copies into its fourth edition.

49   He wrote the obituary of Timothy Thomas Castellnewydd.

50   The second wife was the widow of David Lewis (Cynfin) who survived him by a few months.

51   Echoes from the Welsh Hillside, David Davies. Tentmaker Publications 2002.

52   Obituaries.

53   This was the final assessment by his contemporaries written for his Obituary.

54   James J Ivor, Molleston Baptist Church, Pembrokeshire. Reflections on the Founders Tricenary Lodwick & Sons Carmarthen 1968 p20.

55   Sermons preached in London by Rev W A Griffths, Narberth. Elliot Stock 62 Paternosyer Row, EC. 1880 p8.

56   Narberth, Whitland and Clynderwen Weekly News, Thursday, December 20 1906 p8.

57   Rochester Mary My Father was a Narberth Man. Anne Loader Publications 1998 p15.

58   Narberth Newspaper.

59   Bethesda Baptist 1808-1958 150 Anniversary.

60   Exodus 1 : 8.

61   As Far as to Bethany Printed and Published by Gee & Son Limited Feb 2000 Peter Trumper .

Save your people, O Lord, and bless those who are your inheritance. Since a door large with promise has swung open for the gospel, let your word have free course in every place, and let it be glorified.

Matthew Henry
Baptist Minister and Commentator

Bethesda Chapel

200 Year Anniversary
Chapel image courtesy of Ieuan Williams